The Book of **HAYES**
and the Story of
BIG MOMMA
IN BLACK

The Book of **HAYES** and the Story of **BIG MOMMA** IN BLACK

By Regina G. Ray

The Book of Hayes and the Story of Big Momma, In Black
Copyright ©October 2023
Regina G. Ray

ALL RIGHTS RESERVED

No portion of this publication may be reproduce, stored in any electronic system, or transmitted in any form or by any means, electronic, mechanical, photocopy, recording, or otherwise, without written permission from the author. Brief quotations may be used in literary reviews.

Cover: by Regina. G. Ray

Available at amazon.com

ISBN:978-1-7365935-8-5

Also purchase at amazon.com:
Contemplations In Black
ISBN: 978-1-736935-0-9
Balance In Black
ISBN: 978-1-7365935-1-6
Kwanzaa Year Round
Annual Family Book
ISBN: 978-1-7365935-2-3
Family Fun to Learn Word Find
ISBN: 978-1-7365935-4-7
Journeying Tree of Life Journal
ISBN: 978-1-7365935-5-4
Home Reading Practice
ISBN: 978-1-7365935-6-1

Dedication

This Great Work is dedicated to the Supreme Creator of the first Aeon, and the Divine Mother of Heaven and Earth; Big Momma, whom we seek to restore to her Riteful Throne of Heaven and Earth. We seek also to restore her within our hearts, and family homes for the sake of the children who are our future selves.

This Great Work is dedicated to the many Ancestors who have preceded us today. It is their Great Works upon which we continue to build. Because they took the time to preserve their Ascended Knowledge, we have a clear and solid path to follow.

This Great Work is dedicated to each and every one today who contributes daily to the way, the service, and the expansion of the collective consciousness of ascension as we journey on the 'Path of Liberation' to dwell within the Mer where the keys of Power, Wisdom, and Unity reign supreme.

Everyone is where they SHOULD be right now. Do not think that you or anyone else is not. We each have different roles to fulfill, but we all together will get to where we are going. Live your best life right where you are, as you are and continue the climb to your higher self.

#FREE
LARRY HOOVER
MUMIA ABU-JAMAL
MALIK ANGEL BEY
ASATA SHAKUR
R.I.P. to all of the GEORGE FLOYDS of history

TABLE OF CONTENTS

Profile..	8
Preface..	9
Introduction..	27
The Book of Hayes...	31
George Washington Challenge................................	36
How the Universe Got Hijacked By the Lesser Gods........	80
Reincarnation and the Afterlife...............................	95
Schematic Table of Kemetic Beginnings	106
Yakub Grafted Beings Revisited.............................	114
Yakub: Part 2..	127
Big Momma Energy...	129
How to Do Shadow Work......................................	131
Where Is All the Beef..	164
Appendix: The Tree of Life....................................	200
References	208
About the Author..	210

PROFILE

Seemingly from out of thin air, Rod Hayes. He said that he has been here before, many times even. "I am the elect of my Momma," Big Momma that is. In past times Rod has warred in the sands of the Sahara, before it was sand. He has seen the Gulf and the shores of Louisiana, before the Gulf was present. In this incarnation, he was raised from the red clay of the Mississippi as a country boy. Boy he is no longer. He grew up fast, having faced incarceration at an early age, during which time he received the challenge of his young life – this life that is. His assignment: unscramble some eggs – and he did. In doing so, he has scrambled some brains, but they will be okay with time. There are more pressing matters at hand. While behind bars and as a captive audience to his books, Rod has read all that there is to read and then some. As a result, and with the obvious brilliance of his mind, and tenderness of heart for his people, Rod has put the fictitious, disjointed, dismissive story of the making of the United States in the Americas into a proper and inclusive perspective of factual logic and truth. Our story is no longer his-story. The marginalized organic Natives, particularly the 'Black Americans', now and finally have a clear path, a proper blueprint to unite on. From the words and the God mind of Rod Hayes, here I present to you <u>The Book of Hayes</u>.

Preface

FORCES

Out from the stillness of any point in space, time began. Since this beginning, varying forces have come to be; some that can be seen, and some that cannot be seen. Each force has in common one thing – movement. You too are a force amongst these many forces. There is never a moment when you and these seen and unseen forces are not moving. Such is life.

Life is a collection of many forces moving in concert; all together, in and around one another. This movement is best overstood as a swirl that forms circular patterns. Over time these movements collaborate collectively into circular patterns. Occasionally a force may collide into another force causing sharp and jagged edges that will overtime soften and become smooth. Such is life.

All forces possess intelligence based upon its purpose. When you overstand the purpose of a force, you can better overstand and even predict its' movements. When observed carefully, we come to realized that every force exists within a greater force. Whereas, the greater force has forces that exist inside of it, it too exists inside of something greater than itself. This was the teaching of Dr. Delbert Blair. There are two terms that that describe the relationship between forces:
Macrocosm–larger outer forces
Microcosm – smaller inner forces

Larger does not necessarily translate to stronger; nor does smaller always equate to weaker. The elemental arrangement of a force, and the surrounding arrangements that effect the force determines its strength. Everything is relative based upon environmental and internal conditions.

I take the time to explain carefully in such detail because many people grow from childhood into adulthood oblivious to origins and purpose, and therefore lack awareness of the relationships between forces contained within life.

As humans, we each are a special force of intelligence with purpose. Yet, unlike the Animal Kingdom, we do not possess a keen instinctive sense of purpose. Instead, we have been provided with a special faculty called the 'Will' which is the freedom to observe and determine our own path in life (wherever societal freedoms exist). We enter upon one of two paths – fate or destiny, based on the choices we make.

Fate; is a path of chance – being led without knowledge by external forces

Destiny is a path of purpose – being guided in wisdom and knowledge by internal forces; divinely

KNOWLEDGE

The determining factor between fate and destiny is knowledge. There are degrees of knowledge. An accumulation of knowledge is 'growth.'

Life is indeed a journey of accumulated knowledge that leads to growth.

Every journey has a beginning. Becoming lost in life may be a matter of not having an awareness of your beginning, or not adhering to that which is known of your beginning. This places one at higher risk of journeying on a path of chance that leads to a lesser known fate; to an alternate destination, often unknowingly and predetermined by external forces. Two non-reflective sayings:

"I'll take my chances"
-v.-
"Because I know who I am."

There too is a third view, "Because I know who I am, I'll take my chances," implying a wish to deviate from that which is known.

As for the beginning, there are an infinite number of beginnings because there are an infinite number of forces, each with its own beginning. Within all the points of time and space, the more knowledge of as many of these points you come to know, the better you come to know your own place within the midst of the continuum of space and time. This is called orientation and/or relativity. With proper orientation, you can better contribute to your own 'story-line' on the stage of life. The more knowledge that you accumulate brings you closer to a more comprehensive knowledge of self.

• What of the young man raised without the guidance of a father, who is forced to take his chances, with the support of his Mom of course, and becomes a professional sports player, making millions?

• What of the little girl and her siblings caught in the cycle of welfare with no inheritance to start in life?

• What of the former sharecropper family who are now on their 2nd generation of college degrees?

• What of those who have made it out of the hood through the military to now serve as the highest ranking amongst his or her peers?

• What of those who cycle in and out of prison, and just cannot get a grip?

• What of the rich kid who finds distasteful the lavish, ill-gotten wealth of his family, and thus chooses to set out on his or her own?

• What of the person trying to escape a history of alcoholic parents?

A variety of diverse scenarios exist amongst people; some are based on a lack of education and knowledge that leads to the frustrations of living outside of the mainstream of society. For example, we have situations of people living under less than desirable circumstances while trying to get a foothold in the establishment of a secure and prosperous life; we have babies raising babies; we also have the injustices of an occupying government and military takeover of indigenous lands. These are all challenges that we must continue to work to overcome on both personal and collective levels.

More often than not, however, knowledge and guidance increases the odds of success. I speak of a positive **'family tradition'** of generational knowledge and guidance; I speak of proactive preparations of **'family Inheritance'** as a head-start for our future selves; and the continuation and improvement upon former Ancestral successes of **'clear familial paths with divine purpose'**; guidance that will add up to a proud **'family legacy'** where each generation does not have to start from scratch and fend for themselves. Your future selves must in turn provide for their future selves. This is inclusive of individuals that start new beginnings of family.

This is the process of becoming 'grounded' in purpose, rather than floating about space and time aimlessly. Family maintenance and support is the best way to achieve grounding. There remains room for individuality and creative expression of self along with this commitment to a familial legacy. Proper orientation within a collective unit such as family is the best way to achieve the success of connecting to your path of purpose within the vastness of life.

Continuity, stability, and success can best be achieved with a clear path of purpose within an unbroken line of Ancestral inheritance.

BEGINNINGS

Let's talk more about the scheme of life. Most scientists and philosophers agree that the beginning started as chaos – an unstructured flurry of elemental activity without direction and purpose. African Ancestral knowledge tells us that when time arrived, order came, that led to the need for instructional Principles. Principles gives direction and purpose. The universe was then set upon a constructive course of structured patterns that allowed for creation to happen.

Consider the word 'exist'; based upon intellectual logic and partly upon instinct, along with esoteric intuition, most would agree that a greater intelligence played a part in the greater and intricate complexities of life. It is in this pre-existence where I wish to begin.

Through the course of time, man has used the method of **'personification'** to communicate knowledge of unseen principles and esoteric explanations. Yet, we should not concern ourselves with just any man on this subject. We must get back to the earliest of man to see what this early man recorded of their knowledge on the matters of life. Later recordings are second-hand presumptions. According to First Man, life arose from both masculine and feminine coupled energies working together. This is the basis of the most basic principles in life. 'Manifestation' which is the portal through which creation is formulated is of a feminine energy, thus the word 'exist';

ex-- meaning to exit, and –ist the root of 'sister' together can be translated literally as 'to come out from her." [Karim]   Yet, the inherent tone of the command is that of a masculine nature based upon 'intellect.' Inherent intellect exists behind the design of all creation.

> **Intellect**; the master builder or Father energy designs
> **Manifestation**; the Mother energy berths
> Together, in this cooperative manner, creation comes forth. This equation occurs at all levels of creation; atomic, molecular, mineral, animal, and plant. Collectively the process is referred to as 'alchemy.'

The earliest of human life, according to archeological findings, most probably originated in the Nile Valley, deep within the heart of the 'Motherland.' This too is where the first writings and recordings developed, yet elaborate ancient writings have also been found on the opposite side of the waters. Within the earliest texts, much knowledge was recorded of what the Ancestors knew of the beginning, and they knew a great deal, having arrived with inherent knowledge in hand. If not for their recordings, advancements of today would have surely been delayed.

Of early human existence, 'evolutionists' would have us to believe that human life evolved in the same manner as plants and animals, but the monumental evidence of early human life is much to the contrary. The recorded knowledge received from ancient times is of an ascended nature. Written inscriptions, titles and roles, woven cloths, forged jewelry, monuments unduplicable by modern standards, land, water, and air transportations, cosmic mappings, and more speak to the presence of First Man as an Ancient Ascended people, and we are their descendants.

Still there is more to this story of the beginning. Beginnings imply that there is an end, and we may be closer to this end than we think. The word 'beginning' is often used interchangeably with the word 'genesis.' While we assume 'genesis' to mean 'the first,' in the case of planet Earth, it actually describes 'a beginning.' There have been many beginnings upon Earth. The biblical Adam and Eve date back to only six thousand years ago. Ancient *Kemetic peoples and their monuments date back beyond tens of thousands of years.*[Ancient African Kemet later became the Greek Egypt as invaders encroached]

A PENDING END

Ancient African knowledge tells us that Earth renews itself every 26,000 years by use of one of its' four elements. [AEO] This can be charted easily as a pie-chart:

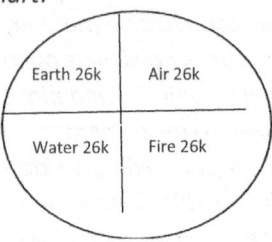

```
        Earth 26k | Air 26k
        ----------|----------
        Water 26k | Fire 26k
```

There is no one living today that was alive 26 thousand years ago. There, however, are myths and signs of a past worldwide flood. Scientists have also worked out the occurrence of past 'Ice Ages' and cataclysms.   Ancient African ancestral knowledge tells us that the next expected Earth renewal will be by fire. [AEO]

Precession: Within Earth's spin pattern there is another rotation that occurs; there is a precession. Earth's axis forms a cone that extends from Earth's core to a distance above the planet where the top of the cone forms a 360 degree pattern (a circle) in the opposite direction of the spin of the Earth, thus the 'Precession' marches through the zodiacal signs in reverse. Like a spinning top, this pattern can be expressed as a 'wobble.' This wobble is called a Precession and it takes Earth approximately 26,000 years to complete this reverse cone pattern. [Chaisson & McMillan]

> An Astrological Age; is a time period in astrology that corresponds to major changes in the development of Earth's inhabitants, particularly relating to culture, society, and politics. An astrological age corresponds to the twelve zodialogical signs. Astrological ages occur because of a phenomenon known as the Precession of the Equinoxes. One complete period of a precession, having passed through all twelve zodialogical signs, is called a Great Year (Jubilee) or Platonic Year of about 25,920 years. [Wikipedia]

We are currently at a point in time when several significant esoteric and geographical events are coinciding.

A. End of the Age of Pisces
B. Start of Age of Aquarius
C. Completion of a Precession
D. Stoppage and reversal of Earth's core
E. An anticipated Reversal of Earth's Polar Poles
F. Inversion of Earth's Torsion Field is then expected

The spinning of Earth's core was reported January 2023 as 'stopped.' What could this mean? The lack of convection movement (an even distribution of earth's core heat) may allow for over-heating at specific locations around the earth, thus resulting in higher than normal thermal activities on the planet's surface. It has been reported in the news that the slowing of the core may have accounted for scientific anomalies over the past 60 – 70 years. If it has taken this long to slow to a halt, re-initiation during reversal may or may not follow this same time frame and we may be in for a bumpy road ahead.

The total number of earthquakes worldwide has increased from approx. 152 earthquakes per decade at the start of the twentieth century, and has been increasing in an exponential manner to 560 earthquakes per decade mid-twentieth century, to 192,204 worldwide in year 2020. Based upon the historical trend of earthquakes, it has been predicted that in year 2028 at least one thousand earthquakes will occur worldwide per year, and by 2036 Earth can experience over a million earthquakes in a year. [Global Crisis Forum]

The above research supports African Ancestral knowledge that has been known within the Ancient Egyptian Order [AEO] of today about Earth's renewal.

> For those who are concerned about getting money, it's not about money. It's about matching your vibration to the earth so that you can reap the benefits of your purpose and share the knowledge of healing and ascension; mental and spiritual ascension. [BDell1014]

A new Age fades in as the next fades out over approximately a 100 year period before coming into its fullness. The predominate energies, during this overlapping period, that ruled the passing age diffuse out, and the characteristic energies of the incoming age phases in. This slow moving transitional anticipation conforms to the constant and steady movement of life.

The Age of Pisces carried a feminine, mutable, and water energy. The Age of Aquarius carries a masculine, fixed, air energy. It was stated in a French news article that Aquarius is in the house of the woman. How Aquarius translates into the age of the woman, I must call upon the assistance of zodiac experts.

***

> Aquarius has to do with the good of the group, personal detachment, and concerns for the eclectic "whole." However, its' opposite, Leo, believes in individual sovereignty, passionate feelings and the ability to decide for oneself the appropriate course of action...Remember, balance is the key. We can find a way for caring for the Earth and all of her inhabitants without sacrificing personal liberties. [Celeste Longacre, April 3, 2023]

***

> The Age of Aquarius marks a new era for humanity as we collectively shift from a patriarchal society to one that incorporates feminine values...We are still in the early stages of this age, but it is already clear that we need to respect our differences to create a more just world for all humankind. This will require us to embrace our inner feminine and honor all the expressions of womanhood. [David's Conscious Identity, November 22, 2022]

***

> The Age of Pisces was (and perhaps still is) a time of escapism – a time when we blind ourselves to the tragedies surrounding us in order to spend more time in our own fantasy worlds. While this can be beneficial in certain moments, Aquarius is asking us to wake up and smell the injustices. [Rhiannon Liselle, July 5, 2020]

***

The Western concept of the dawning of the Age of Aquarius envisions an increase of the feminine influence, the feeling of the pulse of mother earth, and the equality of the sexes (with the woman being just a little more equal). Instead, I believe the present feminine oriented Western society will collapse and/or be blown away and then be replaced by a masculine oriented rebuilding that will strive for the betterment of humankind and a return of an understanding and implementation of the natural patriarchal structure. [Elder George, February 15, 2008]

***

Pisces under a feminine sign, which represents only one side of the balanced equation, must be balanced with the rise of the masculine. This was the basis of the Pope, a masculine Patriarch 'occupying' the Matriarchal Throne of the Earth Mother. However, at the start of the new age, the masculine energy of Aquarius requires the balanced energy of the feminine. Thus, the feminine energy rises to match the incoming masculine energy as the Matriarch re-assumes her throne seat. [Regina Ray, September 3, 2023]

OCCUPY

Up to this new millennia, observing over the course of life and its living in modern America, the relationship between humans and mankind has continued on a destructive path of continued aggression and expansion by the armed and militarized northern Europeans into the Americas. Usurpation and occupation of the Americas and its lands by northerners, away from the organic people of the land have been to the grave detriment of Native Indigenous human life following this continued overall pattern of Colonialism since the 1700s. This includes the spread of northern Spanish and Latin speaking Europeans occupying governmental control over the South, Central, and Island Americas; British, Jewish, French, Scandinavian, German, and Baltic Europeans into North America; the French into what is now called Canada; the Spanish, and British into North, South and Central America. With this comes the forced mental expansion of the foreign Christianity and its theological religious edicts and practices of death, slavery, Christmas and Easter, along with later development of its capitalistic pagan offspring's of Santa Claus and Easter bunny. Resultant consequences have been the whitening and lightening of brown and black southern cultures that has spurn the psychologically detrimental practices of division in all aspects of the resultant society based upon tonal complexion, where such divisions did not previously exist prior to northern influx, thus disturbing the prior social balance of peaceful existence in the Americas. An occupational corporate government referred to as the United States, which is an interwoven matrix of Amorite Law, Commercial Code, in a Democratic, Capitalistic hierarchal organization of theft and corruption; the legalized theft of labor, land, wealth, and resources from the Indigenous Natives of this land; under a Constitution that continues to hold hostage the sons and daughters of the 'Confederate Native Nations of the Republic' imprisoned into the most detrimental conditions of this society. This is just the physical aspect of the torrent history of modern America.

BIG MOMMA

The Story of 'Big Momma' is a revealing story of the esoteric aspects of 'Ourstory.' Big Momma's story is our story and shares the details of how she originated and evolved through the millennia, up to her significance to us today. The new Age of Aquarius signals new beginnings for us all in many ways. The return of Big Momma is the greatest of what the new Age brings.

Her Ancient names are Taweret; Ta-Urt; or Thoueris.[Britannica] She is known as the "Great Female of the Land" She holds the Royal Blood Rites to the Earth. We as 'First Man' and organic man to the Earth are her descendants and heirs. Her ancient personified image can be found at the center of the **Zodiac Disc of Dendera** (a representative 'center of the Universe'). The Kemetic image is of a hippopotami that represents fertility, with the face of a crocodile that represents her ferociousness, and hind legs of a lion that represents her strength and swiftness. She carries in her hand the feather of Maat that represents the principles of righteousness and justice. She represents the Great Mother; Creator in the 2nd Aeon; the Great Feminine; the Great Black; the Primordial Waters from where all arise.

Taweret; In ancient times as the protectress of childbearing women; She was also considered the protectress of infants and children... but venerated for brute strength and staying power, and ability to scare just about anything that shouldn't be present away. [Kemetic Orthodoxy/Kemet.org]

The story of her beginning is found in the **Cosmogony**, the ancient African story of creation as told by the Sages of the Akan, the Yoruba, the Dogon, and Benin peoples.

Pre-Kemetic mythology details our former spiritual existence as a cosmic nature before our souls became trapped into the mortal bodies of the earthly man. These mythological recordings have been preserved in stone and on papyrus leaf by our ancestors from as far back as five thousand B.C. and beyond, to be delivered to us today in this new millennial age. Our story begins on the Sirius star which aligns with the belt of Orion and is in the Canis Major Constellation, an apex of the vast universe and point from which creation commenced.[Contemplations In Black, by R. G. Ray]

Big Momma has evolved throughout the Ages as the dominant controlling force of nature and man. She is seen as **Auset**, the most adored and adorned of all the Earth. In her capacity of Auset, she is the Consort of **Ausar**, Lord of the Great Black; she is the Mother of **Heru** by Immaculate Conception; her hieroglyphic symbol in Kemetic writings (Medu Neter) is the Throne Seat, for she is the Great Mother of both Heaven and Earth. Her story can be found in the **Ausarian Drama** of Kemet. **Key:** Kemetic Name / Greek Name

Kemetic Name	Greek Name
Auset	Isis
Ausar	Osiris
Heru	Horus
Kemet	Egypt
Tehuti	Thoth, Hermes

In addition to the Great Mother and Auset, Big Momma evolved into her continued expansions as the Goddess **Hathor**, also referred to as **Mut-Netcher** (Mother Nature in modern tongue).

> Mut Netcher- Hathor; the Great Mother of the World; Mother Nature; the Great Universal Mother of the Sky Goddess, and dates to pre-dynastic times as she appears on the Narmer palette; she represents the feminine principle; the Cosmic Mother; Lady of the Stars and Universe.
>
> [ancientegyptonline.co.uk]

TIMELINE

As Big Momma fulfils other capacities as Creator in this 2nd Aeon, let us continue her journey into today. Whereas Earthly beginnings have been well documented in the deserts of Kemet, life has been lived out all over the planet. It is this establishment and progression of life on Earth we seek to follow. To establish a proper timeline, there must also be an overstanding that the start of man on Earth was not in Egypt, but within the interior region of today's Africa. The great pyramids of Giza were the latest and last pyramids built. So life migrated from the interior of Africa, up the northern flow of the Nile River into Kemetic Egypt, and throughout the world.

> Evidence of human habitation in Egypt stretches back tens of thousands of years. It was only in about 6000 BCE however, that widespread settlement began in the region. [Khan Academy.com]

The Bible establishes the timeline of Adam and Eve to have occurred approximately 4,000 B.C. There are 76 generations between Adam and Christianity's Jesus. This four thousand years (now six) represents Genesis, or the genetic making of 2nd mankind. The second creation of man occupied the Caucus mountainous terrains of Greece to Rome, and chiseled out other territories across Europa. These mountainous people eventually ventured east, only to find vast empires of mythical proportions engaged in all aspects of civilization, trade, and culture. It was here in Kemetic Egypt that they came to study and learn. It was here that spiritual and cosmic existences were thoroughly incorporated into both the scholarly lives and daily lives of the Kemetic people. It was here too that the Great Throne of Heaven and Earth was highly honored; Big Momma's Seat.

Europe was named after a Black Goddess named Europa. Britannica.com concludes "No one knows for sure the origin of Europe's name, but it certainly stuck"—such is how the eraser of Black History occurs. Wikipedia records indicate two historical figures; 1) Europa of Macedon who was the daughter of Phillip I by his last wife Cleopatra Eurydice. She is widely believed to have been murdered along with her mother by Olympias, Phillip's fourth wife and the mother of Alexander the Great. Ref: Carney Elizabeth Donnelly. <u>Women and Monarchy in Macedonia</u>. Norman, Oklahoma. Pg. 7. ISBN: 0-585-23812-X. OCLC 44954635.

2) Europa, in Greek mythos, a Phoenician princess from Tyre Lebanon and mother of King Minos of Crete, she was abducted by Zeus in the form of a Bull.

Both ancient Macedonia and the ancient Phoenicians (as was ancient Egypt, and Roman/Etruscans for that matter, and Native Americans, etc.) are originally melanated peoples.

The Mediterranean people called the Anu, founded Ancient Crete, which gave birth to the Minoan civilizations, which then spawned Mycenaean civilization, which then fathered ancient Greece... While Europeans gave all credit to Greece and Rome, the Greeks and Romans themselves looked to Ancient Egypt and the Anu people as the true fathers of civilization. [When the World Was Black, vol. 2, Pg. 237]

Medieval Northern man of Europa struggled through many decades, which turned into many centuries of back and forth warring's, dark ages, unsanitary conditions of pestilences and consumption, illiteracy, and internal slavery. Roman military excursions into the east sought to conquer and transfer the most coveted aspects of Kemetic spirituality, wealth, and knowledge west to their leader in Rome, Augustus Caesar. There is much of his-story to study and learn in order to backfill the many holes within this brief review

GREEK GODS

Kemetic recordings document's its high vibrational cosmic beginnings into the transitional low vibratory phase of human life on Earth. Second man, after decades of studying in Kemetic Egypt, decided to adopt aspects of the very real and authentic cosmic stories of Kemet. They changed deity names, and developed their own cosmic rendition called the 'Greek Gods of Olympia' sometime after Homer's <u>Iliad</u> of 800 B.C. This is how the Kemetic Auset became known as the Greek **Isis**, Ausar Lord of the Great Black became **Osiris**, and their son Heru became the Greek **Horus**. Also, the Kemetic Tehuti became the Greek **Thoth, Tresmisgustus,** and **Hermes**. The Greek Gods of Olympia contain an expansive array of characters and tales of Zeus and Olympia, Apollo, Poseidon, Athena, Venus, Prometheus, etc. These tales have evolved over the years to include modern tales of gnomes, fairies, trolls, and many other characters. This too requires extensive study into the great imaginings of the Greeks.

> Shakespeare's poem of "Venus and Adonis" which is at root mythology fleshed in a human form. Again and again the Egyptian Mythos furnishes a prototype that will suffice to account for a hundred Folk-tales…This origin of our Folk-lore may be found a hundred times in the "Wisdom of old Egypt."
> [Gerald Massey, Ancient Egypt-Light of the World, 1907]

Mythology has it that Alexander the Great [357 B.C.–324 B.C.] proclaimed himself to be the son of the mythological Zeus, whereas his mother Olympias was the wife of King Phillip I. Alexander, a Greco-Roman, is recorded as having conducted a lengthy military campaign throughout Western Asia and Egypt around 323 B.C [Wikipedia]

> It is not untrue to say that the Roman Empire, the spread of Christianity as a world religion, and the long centuries of Byzantium were all in some degree the fruits of Alexander's achievement. [Frank H. Walbank and the Editors of Encyclopedia Britannica]

> From a Catholic viewpoint, the primacy of the bishop of Rome is largely derived from his role as the apostolic successor to

Saint Peter, to whom primacy was conferred by Jesus, who gave Peter the Keys of Heaven and the powers of "binding and loosing" , naming him as the 'rock' upon which the Church would be built. [Wikipedia]

Ethiopia contains the earliest known Christian Church. In Rome's desire to become the spiritual center of the world, apart from the eastern spiritual centers of Kemet, Ethiopia, and Jerusalem, the Roman Pope corresponded with Ethiopia urging them to recognize Rome as their spiritual leader and to denounce their Egyptian Coptic ties. The Ethiopian Christian Church sent a reply to Rome as 'not affirmed.' To this day, Catholic robes, head dress, and alter practices mimic that which originated in Ethiopia.

In summary:
1. We have Alexander who lived 300 years before Jesus, as somehow responsible for the spread of Christianity.
2. We have the mythical story of Jesus, without any confirmed biographical documentation of that time outside of the Bible; and with Biblical plagiarisms from Kemetic documentations, such as the Ten Commandments being identical to the Laws of Maat, and the book of Psalms coinciding with the writings of Akhenaten.
3. We have literary character equivalents in Greek mythology written sometime after 800 B.C. that equate to the Kemetic records that are older than 5,000 -10,000 B.C.

Following the convening of the Council of Nicea and the Canonizing of the Bible in 325 A.D., Rome set up shop in the Europa province of present day Italy. The Catholic Church of Rome ruled over all of Europa, as separate city states became more defined over time into their modern age countries. The details that occurred between military excursions of Alexander in Persia and Egypt in 323 B.C., the entering of the Greeks into Egypt, and the 325 A.D. developments of the Roman Catholic Church and Bible, invasions of the Goths and Vandals into Europa from its north, leading into the Dark Ages and then invasions by the Moors, all led from these years into the modern age include many epic tales of conquering wars, crusades, transferences of knowledge, and secret organizational establishments. Behind it all lay the developing strong hand of the Roman Catholic Church, its edicts and doctrines of severe control.

TRANSFERENCES

In the midst of the east to north drama, the esoteric knowledge of Kemet made the journey out of the control of the high priests of Kemet into the hands of foreigners. This transference took place in the form of Papyrus scrolls, through captured high priests, through re-writings, and new writings based on the mythologies gleaned from papyrus scrolls and off of engraved temple and tomb walls of Kemet. The knowledge so enlightened northern lands from Greece to Rome and throughout Europa, that it spurred the imaginations of northern philosophers, astrologers, mathematicians, architects, artists, musicians and more. Late as it was, Europe finally began to emerge out of her dark ages in the Fifteenth century. The awakening of Europe, meant the death of both Kemetic Egypt first, and then Greek Egypt. She had been drained of her people, spirit, wealth, and life that spilled out like Blood from her veins, enriching the four corners of the Earth, leaving only the dry walls of her temples, pyramids, grand statues, and great edifices, and hidden tombs, standing in the desert.

Another monumental spiritual loss of Kemet was the Royal Seat of Auset; the Throne of the Great Mother of Heaven and Earth, and Big Momma with it. In truth, Big Momma is not someone you can easily lose. You must look for her in her new formations. Big Momma has continued to be upheld worldwide by all of the peoples of the world. To name a few: In Hindu she is known as Shakti; in Caesar's Rome as Bona Dea; her Orisha manifestations are, Oshun, Yemaya, Nana Buruku; Ishtar in Babylon; as Inana in Sumer; as Ezili Dantor in Haiti; she is known as the Ma Donna, the Magna Marta, Isis, Mary, and Jesus (IESOUS) in the north. In recent times Big Momma has been identified in less mythical and mystical terms as she prepares to resume her Throne Seat, and as the new Age of Aquarius comes into its fullness. The question is, where has the throne of Big Momma been located all of this time? The answer to this question is revealed in the **Book of Hayes** that is recorded here for your personal journey into the esoteric knowledge of Our Story. I will state however that:

Rebellion began in the heavens and got its start at Earth's beginning with the first born son; the deity of 'Set.' The rebellion was against the feminine Mother energy. This has become man's greatest challenge from the start. Since the earliest times of this rebellion, the Earth has oscillated back and forth between Matriarchal rule and Patriarchal rule. It is the feminine energy who berths and nurtures the whole of creation. Religions that implement Patriarchal systems around the globe typically oppress the feminine energy. Perhaps Set serves the purpose of Earth's 'necessary evil.'

Characters in Earth's Great Drama include:
The Unchanging Creator in the first Aeon
The Great Mother of creation in the 2nd Aeon
The First Son in his many evolutionary forms - Set, Dagan, Baal, Enlil, Enki, Allah, Jesus, Yahweh, Elohim, Jehovah, Nyonkopon, Obatala, Wakan-Tonka, the Pope, etc.

Patriarchal Religions & Systems of Earth:
Pharaohnic rulers, Babylon, Judaism, Christianity, Sufism, Islam, Zen, Chen, Zoroastrianism, Sikhism, Freemasonry, Buddhism, Taoism, Vatican, KKK, Police, Military, Democratic & Republican parties, Gangs, Mob, Governments, Secret Societies, etc.

Engagements of Patriarchal Religions & Systems:
Worship = war-ship
Corruption and Theft = of land, wealth, labor
Control = ego & power, drugs, trafficking, genocide
Criminalization = imprisonment for profit, and political gains
Suppression of women = physical and mental violations

Even in the absence of her throne, Big Momma's duties continued to be honored and carried out amongst the organic Indigenous peoples of today by Matriarchal spirits such as Winnie Mandela, Imelda Marcos.

Min. Farrakhan and Khadijah with Winnie Mandela   President Ferdinand & Imelda Marcos

There are many organic Matriarchal Chiefs currently in the Americas today working hand in hand with their Brothers to secure the land and maintain the native cultures of the land. The spirit of Unity and collective consciousness continues to grow as the Indigenous people assume their responsibilities to clean and protect the Earth from the enemies who seek to destroy her.

Historical Timeline:
-Contractual reign of Satan = 6K years (from 4,000 B.C. – 2,000 A.D.)
-# of Generations between Adam (2nd man) and Jesus =76 gen. = ~4K yrs.
-Age of First Man = >10K years

First Man	*Genesis Man	Year AD1	Year 2000 /Year 2160
>10K BC	4,000 B.C.	76 gen. from Adam	End of Reign of Satan
Pre-dynastic	Biblical Adam	Start of Pisces Age	/End of Pisces Age
Kemet	6K yr. Reign		/Start of Aquarius Age
>4,500 B.C.	of Satan		

*Date times according to the Gregorian calendar

Is it of coincidence that a recent line of related events have taken place? Such events that have coincided with the end of the six thousand year reign of Satan is:

- Six thousand years since Adam and Eve
- End of a 1492 Bible Contract via Babylonian Blood Magic
- End of a Blood Rite (Death) Oath
- The close of the Piscean Age / Dawn of Aquarius Age
- The end of a 26 thousand year Precession (The Great Jubilee)
- United Nations Declaration on the Rights of Indigenous People September 13, 2007 Resolution 61/295
  (Rejected by the United States and Canada, and Australia)
- *American Declaration on The Rights of Indigenous People June, 15, 2016, AG/RES.2888 (XLVI-O/16) U.S. and Canada
- The death of Queen Elizabeth of England

- The death of Daddy Bush – King George of the west
- The near pending death of Senate leader McConnell
- The appearance of Rod Hayes

The head demons of Satan are dying off; the advent of a New Age and Great Jubilee means the end of all contracts and treaties, return of all lands and wealth to their riteful owners, including Big Momma's Throne Seat of Heaven and Earth.

*Earth Rites; your organic Rite is to your land of Heritage and Birth. Earth Rites are divinely imparted; no government of man can give it. Government of man can offer only Constitutional and Civil Rights.

INTRODUCTION

You know the story, or at least you did once when you dwelt on the other side. Other side you ask? When the mind is expanded in knowledge beyond the five senses, you will experience the reality of life in its entirety, not just that which you know through family photo albums, or black and white flics of television and movies. It is through knowledge and true divine impartation that an awareness of seen and unseen realities lift one from lowly carnal concerns into monumental heights of immortal perception. One can walk through life looking down at their feet and lower parts with an occasional horizontal glance across a table or across the street. Or, instead, gain a universal perception from a cosmic view of what was, what is, and what is to be. The latter was our perception on the other side, prior to entering the portal of the womb to arrive onto this physical plane.

We must rewind time to learn of the first womb; the womb of Big Momma. Hers is the same womb that persists today, for it has multiplied from the one to the many. A search that begins from this starting point of the beginning will lead us through epic tales of yesteryears, of how time has unfolded, and how we have landed, or have always existed as we are and where we are today. Big Momma's memory is long and she keeps count of her children. She wishes us well in our endeavors, but does not fail to punish when we are out of order. In this way she shows her love, while not violating the universal principles that she has provided for us all to live and enjoy life by. To know and obey your original Momma; your first Momma is your way back to the eternity from where you came.

This physical realm is experienced through our five senses of sight, hearing, touch, smell, and taste. The spiritual realm is beyond our five senses and requires a greater awareness. Big Momma resides in both realms. As humans, we too reside in both provided that we have the proper knowledge and awareness. Just the same as Big Momma, we have responsibilities to uphold in this game of life. Big Momma has a celestial throne that floats between both realms. However, her throne was usurped from her by an adversarial opponent; a throne to which she seeks a return. Her return is incumbent upon you and I and our awareness first of Big Momma in our lives, and secondly, the condition of her throne.

In order to conceive the presence of Big Momma, you must first conceive your own true reality, aside from the physical realm. Earth is surrounded by an electro-magnetic *'Torsion Field'* that is responsible for the containment of our atmosphere. Vital atmospheric gases are held beneath the surrounding containment field, while cosmic bodies and debris is held outside of the field. This physical yet invisible magnetic field is generated by the flow of electrons within and around Earth's two *Polar Poles*. Ions carry a positive charge at one end and a negative charge at the opposite end. This ionic column makes up Earth's North Pole region and

South Pole region. As a diagram, the magnetic field is in the shape of a donut with the hole at Earth's center and surrounds the earth like a cage with longitudinal and latitudinal lines. Spiritually, this magnetic field behaves much like a black hole that seeks to draw you in as it collapses in upon itself. The more and denser one becomes attached into this physical world, they fall into this state of being consumed. Know, that each thing you consume in this world, it too consumes you. Don't walk too heavy in your shoes. Walk lightly, free your mind from those things that weigh you down, liberate yourself. This is what it is to be spiritual. Spirituality is a liberating energy that unbound you from physical entrapments on this physical plane.

The physical world seeks to cover and consume the spiritual realm; to draw in the spiritual world as the physical world collapses in on itself. This is the struggle of the indigenous peoples around the planet, to not be consumed by those who for centuries have continued their onslaught of deposing us from our lands, culture, truth, ourselves, and from one another; consumption by vampirism; culture vultures. Spirituality is our highest and greatest power, yet least familiar to us. When you are spiritually in touch with self, then you are in touch with your Ancestors, the creation, and the Creator.

Until now, we have been educated based upon what has been put before us; that which was prepared by others, not toward our benefit. It is essential that we prepare educational materials tailored toward our targeted goals that bring collective benefits to self. There is *Ancient African Ancestral Knowledge* available that can assist us collectively in this journey called life, for those who wish to start their spiritual journey. These include:

1. Ancient African Ancestral Knowledge
2. A Kwanzaa Story
3. The African "Cosmogony"
4. The Kemetic Ausarian (Osirian) Drama
5. The 42 Laws of Maat
6. The Tree of Knowledge
7. The Tree of Life
8. The Seven Laws of Tehuti (Thoth) / Universal Principles
9. The Emerald Tablet

* Refer to: *Contemplations In Black; Balance In Black; Ancient African Ancestral Knowledge In Black;*
@amazon

The world has two systems running; a *Matriarchal* system, and a *Patriarchal* system. The planetary Native Tribes of the Indigenous peoples traditionally adhere to the Matriarchal system, while the non-indigenous operate from a Patriarchal system. The Patriarchal system is spread throughout the world by two methods; *1) politically by democracy; and 2) via Christianity.*

Complex happenings over time have been studied and brought together in a comprehensive manner for the first time in modern history. Here, the facts are displayed as given in *The Book of Hayes.*

The Book of Hayes

Restoration of the Great Cosmic Mother

1. De Vatican is really the house of the *Divine Feminine; Grand Matriarch* of the planet. They moved the location from Kemet to Rome when Rome took power. They had 6K years to rule, because they could only hold that seat until the woman comes back for her power at the close of the age. This involves the *'Shrine of the Black Ma Donna.'* The Pope wears white. The *Great Mother* wears black. The sisters they call the *'Nuns'*, we call them *Sisters of the Nūn*. The Nūn in white was the mirror opposite of the *Primordial Nūn; The Great Waters* where all things spring from. The closest example of what occurred is seen in the story of Cleopatra.

2. Two thousand years ago they said Jesus got crucified for being a heretic. You have to look closely at what's contemporary with the time frame. The Greek language writes Jesus as 'IESOUS.' Rules of grammar, this spells 'ISIS.' The story of Jesus is the divine sacrificing of *Venus* the divine feminine. The Pope cannot sit on Big Momma's [Isis] seat; *'The Seat of Isis'* – so he puts his seat under hers.

3. Big Momma's seat is [suspended] about 30 feet over the Pope's seat. The *Daughters of Isis* are the *Cybele (grk.) Sisters* of the high ranking Priest's. This is where you get your heirs to the seat that the Pope is undermining, so they switch the dress of the Nuns to black, and the Pope to white.

4. Isis travels the world to get the support of her Priestesses to back her in her return. That has already been done. We know who the Black Madonna is on the land. All signs point to Khadijah Muhammad [Farrakhan] as the Priestess

Madonna on the land. It is hard to get in touch with her because of who she is.

The Seat of the Matriarch – the only one that is permitted to sit in the seat is the most loved, most respected out of all the Matriarchs on the planet.

5. Alexander of Greece conquered Egypt (Alexander is the son of Zeus; Zeus is Enlil). Enlil's children came to subvert and steal the Rites of the Earth-born. They are stealing the Birth Rite of the woman. To restore the seat back to honor and prominence, everywhere you look around the world, there is a suppressed *Great Mother* – which takes us to the **Magna Marta**, which means *Great Mother*. The *Great Mother* seat is also called the Black Madonna seat, but there is no Black Madonna sitting in it. We must unravel the codes to put the *Great Mother* back on her seat. The Magna Marta produces something call the **Magna Charta** which means the *Great Charta* under King John. The **Magnus Opus** means the *Great Work* is represented by the four Kings of the north, east, south and west – the four winds that raises the fifth Kingdom or seat of the *Great Mother*. There were three who were crucified. One got away and has to come back to claim the other three. This fourth one is the 'little Drummer Boy' – the return of the Messiah.

6. These are all included in the codes of the Masons. In the end, there will be four *Chiefs (Kings)* to come together to raise the throne of the *Great Mother* (four Kings = four corners of Earth = the four winds). The Seven Seas come in by the forces of the four winds. Seven=33+33+33+1/3. The fallen Kings [are the] four animals in the book of Revelation; 1.bull, 2.eagle, 3.lion, 4.Red-long face drummer boy. The *Great Mother* is restored when the *Great Work* is complete.

7. The *Divine Mother* is the *Divine Shakti* (Hindu). *Shakti*=the power of the feminine. The manifestation of *Oshun, Diana, Ishtar, Inana*. Earthborn children have been deposed from their Matriarchal thrones by Patriarchal dominant cultures; i.e. *Enki's* children (Organics) deposed by *Enlil's* children.

8. *Cybele's* who stand in 10 arches, are oracles known for their accuracy of prophesy. There are 12 multicultural *Cybeles* (originally 10 but Inana berthed 2 more daughters), 12 signs of the zodiac (Virgo and Scorpio use to be one, and there was no Libra), and [they] represent the *Sefirot* of the Kabbalah *Tree of Life*. [In the book of] Genesis, enmity [was] put between His seed and Her seed. This was between Scorpio and Virgo. The goal is to get balance back between the two. This represents the imbalance between the sexes.

9. Rebalancing causes a rebalancing of the *Scales of Maat* to eliminate the injustices caused. The zodiac represents the 'Round Table.' At the *Black Dot* center sits the– the 13th*Seat of the Nūn*. The *Primordial Nūn* qualities were personified separately by pairs of Deities. These zodiac pairs = 6 mirror images = 12. There used to be 10 Decans originally, prior to the 12 zodiac signs. Decan means ten. 'Bey' also means 10. Ten mothers are needed to seat a clan chief. This takes us to Gorgon; Gorgon's leader was Medusa. Medusa = 10 in hieroglyphics and looks like an archway.

Medusa is a rank or title. In Greece her name was Helen—*Sa Priestess; Doula*; she was sent to Crete to civilize Greece and build a university.

10. Big Momma was also known as *Taweret* and whose hieroglyphic symbol is a vagina with two legs open [or a portal; as a looped ribbon]. *Venus of Willendorf* as the oldest worshiped statue [relic] in Europe is [from] 30 thousand years ago. The Bible says [that] Earth is only 6 thousand years old.

Mother Claire Muhammad   Mother Khadijah Farrakhan   Sister Donna Farrakhan

11. The *Black Madonna* came through the shrine located at 7625 Linwood Street in Detroit Michigan. Ma means Mother, Donna means Daughter. Who founded the *'Shrine of the Black Madonna?'* It was founded 1967 by *Albert B. Cleage Jr.* The mural wears blue with a white head dress scarf holding a baby wrapped in pink. The heir is a girl. Comes through the Blue House or Father line. The *Nation of Islam Mosque #1* is a Red House. *Fard Muhammad* founded the Nation of Islam. Elijah's wife was *Claire Muhammad*. That means that the *Nation of Islam* is *Claire Muhammad's* daughter. One of her daughters must take her spot. *Claire* was alive when the mural was drawn. Remember that there is a lot of Mommas needed to put a Momma into a *Seat of High Priestess*. *Claire* is the mirror opposite of *Fard Muhammad*, tying the *Madonna* to the land by the flag. [The] credited maker of the American flag is *Betsy Ross*. The original flag had 13 stars in a circle, [which] equals the *Great Mother's Seat and Seal*. *Betsy Ross* was promoted as a role model for all young girls

and woman contributions; [as] a Patriarch role model. *Betsy Ross* had seven children; 7=G=*Circle Seven*.

12. *Khadijah Farrakhan's* birth name is '*Betsy Ross*' and she is now the *First Lady of the Nation of Islam*. [The] daughter of *Minister Farrakhan and Khadijah* name is *Donna*. She would be the heir of Khadijah. The *Ice Princess* comes from the underworld of the *North Gate* of the *Iroquois*.

13. Big Momma's House was the Long House. The Red House was for women. The Blue House was for men. The Constitution was a Blood Rite Oath. The Constitution was stolen and rewritten in the Blood of *Crispus Attucks*, a *Wapanos Native* descendant. It was a *Babylonian Blood Magic Ritual*. This is the contract we are locked into in the Blood of the righteous; located at the George Washington Memorial. (You can see the ink the Constitution is written in is reddish)

14. We are also under a 400 year *1492 Bible Contract*. Babylonian Blood ritual is the maintenance of the contract. Enlil's children were lovers of sin, Blood, sex, money magic, and Marduk (General of chemical warfare) use ritual magic. Fear is an angel repellant. The Blood of the righteous shall not be killed in vain.

15. A lot of the guys do not overstand it and they think it's a bad idea to put the Matriarch back together, but what they don't know it is ran with the children as the first order of business for the next seven generations. The mothers have to consider that in all of their political decisions. Once they overstand that, it will change his divine interactions with the divine feminine, which will change his interactions with women.

16. The value of men with women will vary based upon your personal development. You cannot be a high value target doing low value –ish. You can't do low value –ish and expect to get a high value mate.

Young Elder; "When you treat her like a Queen, then she will treat you like a King and both will come out on top."

Rod; People have a slave mentality about relationships and that is why they do not overstand the nature of the species. Men and women don't function mentally and psychologically the same. The woman wanting the man to behave like a woman breeds a homosexual culture. The man wants the woman to be his homeboy, but she is your counter balance that balances the relationship [not your homeboy]. Don't look at the gloom of yesterday.

GEORGE WASHINGTON CHALLENGE
Rod Hayes & Young Elder

17. *Guest: Dr. Kia Pruitt* on *Raising the Vibration of the Planet*; "The planet must have world peace in order to ascend as a planet. The gold standard is God's standard. Louche is the psychic energy of low vibration that nefarious entities eat. Get your crown in order."

Rod: The organic people realizing their crown, the vibrational shift will bring the gold and silver wealth. The louche energy is very dense in Haiti because they haven't closed the war conjure. The war conjure will close when they have the *State Recognition Ceremony* for the *Oshun Priestess* that was sacrificed for the success of that conjure which opened up that louche cesspool. Everyone in Haiti is not poor. They have gated communities in Haiti. This is what's suspicious to me. The first place that *Christo Columbo the Cologne* landed was Hispaniola. This is the Dominic of Haiti. That's where it all started, and that has got to be where it all ends. So we are moving the vibrational frequencies, riding the energy waves of the weather, the movement of the animals, the alignment of the stars, and the UV-rays that are coming into awaken the dormant DNA to allow our frequency to elevate. This is the planetary ascension.

18. So how they have been keeping this energy going is through mass slaughter, what we call slaughter houses. This is [their] Babylonian Blood magic, the purpose of Babylonian Blood magic is to make the women go into a stupor. [The stupor] is an angelic defense system. Large amounts of the pheromone produced by fear causes the women to know it is not safe, so they turn back their energy to match the regular units. So now the enemy can't see them. They are cloaked. When we give the women back their rituals and their practices to tell them the instructions on how to move the energies back to the original point [prior to] when the drama started.

19. It started in 1492. It's [been] a 500 year war [until now] a protractive struggle. Circumstances of the conflict changed from warfare with a continuous Bloodletting phenomenon based on the Babylon Blood magic. If you go to the place of *Jekyll Island*, they talk about the Federal Reserve, but they don't tell you that they use the energy of our Ancestral burial ground by building structures on top of the burial sites of the most powerful Chiefs that walked the land that so happen to be buried in what they call *Jekyll Island*. Pull the veil back and Dr. Jekyll is the alter ego for Mr. Hyde. He is hiding behind a veil of secrecy. Pull the curtain back and find that all this time the wizard is a little man that has been driving Big Momma's ship without her permission. Now we have put the wizard on notice to evict him from Big Momma's cockpit [helm] and reclaim the Earth for the Earth-born.

20. The *Earth Rites* goes to the women. The mitochondrial sync to the planet which goes back to that ascension. They came over here 500 years ago because they got kicked out of Europe by the *Algonquians* who went to the *Iberia Peninsula* to aid in the turmoil that was going on with the Priesthood. When they got kicked out of Europe, they came over here [to the Americas]. They look like us, but they are not us. All of the people who know that we look alike can't tell us apart. Only one of us are going to realize the that we are two different people occupying the same place, using catch terms that classify us together as a single entity; terms like 'Moor' and 'Cherokee.' They use these terms to stomp out the organic people of the land like we don't know our legacy.

21. Notice that in the George Washington Memorial, there is a display of 'Fezzes', but there is no record of the 'Feathers.' Because they are claiming first Rite to the Birth-Rite to the land because George Washington said that we won't be able to tell in 200 years who is who.

> ***George Washington Challenge:*** *If we would agree to take the fezzes and turbans off the Moors heads and remove the sandals from their feet and enforce severe punishments, and to also swear a death oath between ourselves to religiously and faithfully not to allow anyone to teach the Moorish children who they really were of who their forefathers were, and only allow the Moorish children to be taught that they were truly Negroes, Black people, and colored folks, 200 years from today the Moorish people would not know their nationality nor the national name of their forefathers, also they would not know from which land or Ancestors that they are descendant from.*

21. This came out of the Masonic records of the *George Washington Masonic Memorial*. This was the challenge between the [Indigenous] ones who wear the feathers, and the ones who wore the fezzes. The fezzes belong to the Moors who came from Spain under the penalty of death – which we will get to their Blood oath in a minute. The sword on their heads [fezzes] represents the penalty of death if they betray the oath. But we can discover it as one of the Chiefs on the land and tell our people without consequence. So these are the dirty players. One of the fezzes belong to the translator for *Lewis and Clark [Expedition]*. [Another belonged to *Benjamin Banneker* or *'Big Ben Bey'*, the surveyor of the District of Columbia].

22. In the reading of the George Washington challenge, you will notice that the feathers is missing conspicuously from the challenge. [Where it states:] "And remove the sandals from their feet," Moors didn't wear sandals over here. That is the challenge. Can we tell the difference of what side of the water we belong on? We wore moccasins, and they called moccasins sandals in European tongue. So when they say sandals, they are talking about us, because we are the ones who are supposed to walk free on the land. This ties back to the 400 years contract under the Bible—nailing of the feet of Christ to the cross so that they cannot traverse the freely. "Enforce severe punishment" is the most critical aspect of it [the Challenge]. The enforcement of severe punishment is to create psychic drama that carries on for generations until it self-perpetuates. "And also swear a death oath amongst ourselves to religiously and faithfully not allow anyone to teach the Moorish children who they really were and who their forefathers were, and only allow the Moorish children to be taught that they were truly Negroes, black people, and colored folks." Here, they use the 'Moorish people' as a

catch term. We have to remember that because they are mixing a group of Indigenous Tribes called the Amaru, with the French contingent known as the Mare. But they are all melanated and they look like us.

23. The conjure that they are talking about in the George Washington Challenge was the Feathers vs. the Fezzes. The war bonnets were kept by the older women in Mexico while this is going on. They are still down there waiting to return the Chiefs back to their feathers. But we have to overcome the confusion of us vs. the ones that came in to permanently replace us; those called the 'Dirty Moors.' The ones called the 'Righteous Moors' are the ones who stand in the position of right. We are organically synced to the land of the Americas. We can't go anywhere because we are going to pop right back up when we die; right over here on the same longitude and latitude that we are supposed to come back [return] in. The confusion of who we are — are we Conquistadors or are we Washington Donquistamousers? What are we? Did we get kicked out of Spain or were we already here? This was the question.

24. Which takes us to *Albert Pike,* author of the **Morals and Dogma**; blueprint to execute the protocols of Zion:

> "Masonry, like all religions, conceals its secrets from all except the adepts and sages, or the elect, and uses false explanations and misinterpretations of its symbols to mislead those who deserve only to be misled. The 'blue degrees' are but the outer court of portico of the temple. Part of the symbols are displayed there to the initiates, but he is intentionally misled by false interpretations. It is not intended that he should understand them, but it is intended that he shall imagine that he understands them. Their true

explication is reserved for the Adepts; the Princes of Masonry."

25. So right here what Albert Pike (KKK from Spain) is going over that even their very own, they lack, and if you are not one of the Princes, then you are not worthy to receive the right information. So in this case the adepts of this land was the full feathered Chiefs. *The Great Pequot Slaughter* that became known as *'Black Friday'* was on the heels of our *Harvest Festival of the Chiefs*. It was a final harvest festival of the year after the *Pumpkin Festival* which became Halloween.

26. So now in the *Morals and Dogmas* they map out three world war scenarios:

> *"The third world war must be fomented by taking advantage of the differences caused by the 'agentur' of the 'illuminati' between the political Zionists and the leaders of the Islamic world. The war must be conducted in such a way that Islam, the Moslem Arabic world and political Zionism (the state of Israel) mutually destroy each other."*

This is what you see in the news of Netanyahu of Israel making the alliance with the Saudis. This is the illusion. What it is called is 'shifting the rooks' on the chess board. You shift the rooks to confuse the people. All the time, they have been working together, even when it looks like they were fighting. The Zionists was the *Moor Zionist Temple* over here in the early 1900s that was infiltrated by *Noble Drew Ali* to tell us.

Moorish Zionist Temple

Moors Science Temple; Noble Drew Ali at fore center

27. This is the picture of the **Moors Zionist Temple of New Jersey**(left) around the early 1900s. You can see that they are melanated beings with wooly hair, but they are few in number. This picture is from Nobel Drew Ali, to draw the comparative analysis, for we are the many and they are the few. If you look at the **Moors Science Temple**(right), when Noble Drew Ali came to get the secrets out, you will see that his congregation is huge compared to the picture of the little congregation above.

28. The messages are put in the photographs to tell the story to the posterity, the children to come. They didn't have instamatic cameras and cell phones back then. To take a photo back then was called an 'event.' You see that they are the many [2nd photo]. The ones with their hands in the front is symbolizing the ones that are going to come in off the left bump and they are going to hold their hands together like this while we struggle to get free. Noble Drew Ali says "Don't worry about it," because you see that he doesn't have a glove on his right hand. "Don't worry about it, I'm going to put the secrets in the open." "I have the Master's grip, the Lion's grip." That's what that means.

42

29. Now if you look to the right of him, you will see that the first guys hand is concealed, but if you look at the imprint where his arms are, his arms are overlapping. This means that the right side – the Father line is flipping a secret to the left side – the Mother line, and the secret is for the Mother line to put it in her lap off the left bump – put it out in the open for them to see it. "Let me see your hands," so she puts them on her lap. So all of their regalia is telling you that their affiliations and the schools of thought that they incorporate into discovering the fraud. She [also] has her legs crossed; that is representing the x-chromosomal mitochondrial DNA, [and] she is flipping the secret back to the Father line on the stepchild flip. That why her legs are crossed, but his are straight. He flipped the secret to the Mother line off the Father line and she kicked it back on the cross of the legs flip. The legs is the child and the stepchild. So she is flipping the stepchild on the Father line. [The] keys are out in the open.

30. This is how you read the story. So all of them coming together [are] telling me where I am going to search for the knowledge. I see a fez, I see turbans, but I don't see any feathers. So he is saying that the knowledge is being kept from the Feathers; and he is identifying in here several different key lodges that are involved in keeping the secret from us. He is identifying the *Ancient Arabic Nobles of the Mystic Shrine.* He is identifying *The Moorish Zionist Temple.* He is identifying the *York and the Scottish Rites.* We have been infiltrated in all of the houses. This is what the picture is telling us. Malcom-X exposed – Farrakhan rebuilt.

31. So now with the secret out in the open that we have been infiltrated in all of the houses, this is where the infiltration comes in that "They look like us, but they are not us." In Freemasonry, when their hands are on the outside,

that means that "I am exposing what they are telling us to keep secret." When the gloves are on, they are keeping the secret. When the gloves are off the secret is revealed in the public. Now we just have to find them [the secrets] – it's a *'scavenger hunt.'* It's a *'cannon ball run,'* and the cannon ball came from Spanish ships called the *'Spanish Amada.'* What are they doing over here? Ask *Cortez*, he said that they are looking for the *City of Gold*; and they stole all of our gold. Then they put it on reserve in Switzerland and was borrowing against our gold in order to float the *Federal Reserve Note*. Once they took it [the notes] off the gold standard, they put it on the *'Flat Debt Standard'*; what is known as *'Fractional Reserve Banking.'*

32. So, now they can keep us from ever accumulating any semblance of wealth by making us use *'Credits'* and *'Debits'* in the form of paper currency that is not backed by any substance. If everyone stop paying off loans and stop taking new loans, that will automatically destroy the Federal Reserve. It's already closed. Donald Trump closed it, then he put the duties of the Reserve under the U.S. Treasury Department. The U.S. Treasury Dept. was Big Momma's Bank.

33. About the Blood Oath, under the George Washington Challenge, the Catholic Church gave the orders to shed the Blood under the *'White Man's Burden.'* The **Jesuit Oath** is similar. The Jesuits take this oath for the *Jesuit Society*.

> *"I further more promise and declare that I will; when opportunity presents, make and wage relentless war, secretly or openly, against all heretics, Protestants, and Liberals, as I am directed to do, to extirpate and exterminate them form the face of the whole earth and that I will spare neither age, sex or condition, and*

that I will hand, waste, boil, flay, strangle, and bury alive these infamous heretics, rip up the stomachs and wombs of their women and crush their infant's heads against the walls, in order to annihilate forever their execrable race. That when the same cannot be done openly, I will secretly use the poisoned cup, the strangulating cord, the steel of the poniard or the leaden bullet, regardless of the honor, rank, dignity, or authority of the person or persons, whatever may be their condition in life, either public or private, as I at any time may be directed so to do by any agent of the Pope or superior of the brotherhood of the holy faith, of the Society of Jesus."

34. This is the orders that they were using for the Salem witch trials. This is about these Big Mommas who were teaching 'syncing to the earth' to the European servants and slaves that were brought over here when they came.

The Pope issued the most **Bloody Oath** of the past:
ANIMADVERTIONS
ON THE
Papils Most Wicked
AND
Bloody Oath of Secrecy

For the murdering of Kings, Princes, and slaying of people... (read on google). This is the marquee statement for the application of the *'White Man's Burden' by Roger Kipling*. In relationship to the organic people of the land [planet] whom they call the 'Infidels' and 'peasants', he was good friends with *Cecil Rhoads* who was given the army by the Dutch to settle the African Congo [Leopold of the Belgians too, was of the most detrimental participant to the people of the African Congo].

35. In order to overstand the 'White Man's Burden,' you must first know who is [and what] a *'white man'* means. When they first came over here [to Americas], they were melanated beings, but they called themselves Dutch, Portuguese, French, Englishmen, Spanish, Conquistadors, and Black-a-Moors.

> **[Black's Law Dictionary 4th Edition Pg #868:**
> **FREE WHITE PERSONS.** *"Free white persons" referred to in the Naturalization Act as amended by Act July 14, 1870 has meaning naturally given to it when first used in 1 Stat.n103, c. 3, meaning all persons belonging to the European races then commonly counted as white, and their descendants, including such descendants in other countries to which they have emigrated.*
>
> *It includes all European Jews, more or less intermixed with people of Celtic, Scandinavian, Teutonic, Iberian, Latin, Greek, and Slavic descent. It includes Magyars, Lapps, and Finns, and the Basques and Albanians. It included the mixed Latin, Celtic-Iberian, and Moorish inhabitants of Spain and Portugal, the mixed Greek, Latin, Phoenician and North African inhabitants of Sicily, and the mixed Slav and Tarter inhabitants of South Russia. It does not mean Caucasian race, Aryan race, or Indo-European races, or the mixed Indo-European, Dravidian, Semitic, and Mongolian people who inhabit Persia. A Syrian of Asiatic birth and descent will not be entitled to become a naturalized citizen of the United States as being a free white person. Ex parte Shahid, D.C.S.C., 205 F, 812, 813 United States v. Cartozian...Nor a native-born Filipino. U.S. v. Javier, 22 F 2d 879, 880, 57 App. D.C. 303. Nor a native of India who belonged to Hindu race. Kharaitf Ram Samras v. United States...*
>
> **FREE**
> *Right to go on land again and again as often as may be reasonably necessary. Thus, in the case of a tenant entitled to emblements.*

FREE MEN. *Before the Norman Conquest, a free man might be a man of small estate dependent on a lord. Every man, not himself a lord, was bound to have a lord or be treated as unworthy of a free man's right. Among free man there was a difference in their estimation for Wergild. See Liber Homo.*

FREEDMAN, *IN Roman law, one who was set free from a state of bondage; an emancipated slave. The word is used in the same sense in the United States, respecting Negroes who were formerly slaves. Fairfield v. Lawson, 50 Conn. 513, 47 Am. Rep 669; Davenport b. Caldwell, 10 S.C. 333.]*

For those who don't know, after the wars with Hannibal, they exiled all of a sizable portion of the melanated population to the [Iberian] Isle to try to stamp out the Etruscans, which are the Moors in Italy.

36. 'White man' does not mean Caucasian people [as it has come to mean nowadays]. It does not mean Aryan race, or Indo European races. Nor the Dravidian, Semitic and Mongolian people. These are the ones they brought over here to pass off as the $5 Indians. Now they tell you exactly who they are. If you know who they are in history, you know who they are today. It is clear as day that it does not mean Caucasian race.

Image from cover of *African Presence in Early Europe* by Ivan Van Sertima

37. Everybody not entitled to be categorized as a 'free white person' is by default 'Black,' which is a chess term. In chess the white always goes first. Chess is a Moor's game, and I

don't see any pale faces. The Moor is a 'free white person' in law because the law does not apply to him. He is the one who is the *wielder of law* and the *tool of oppression*. [Pale faces sit in their stead to enforce the oppression].

38. Slavery is a misnomer; it's a cover story to conceal the Conjure War. The slavery was never true.
Ref.; *Davy Walker's Appeal* – an investigation into the brown skin people who looked like us that was in bondage, but wasn't us; an anomaly on the land. It was an artificial history from the George Washington Challenge when they were supposed to treat us harshly for two hundred years. The slave narrative was to try to convince us that we weren't from this land, and the Dirty Moors to say "we are the Chiefs over here." So, the challenge was fezzes (Black) vs. feathers (Black). Chattel slavery as we have been taught did not happen.

39. They took Big Momma's name off her house and 'Big Momma's House' became 'the Big House.' [When] the fez is [angled] to the right [on the head], the tassel is to the right. That means that he bumped the Moors for the fez and the one that he bumped was high ranking. That is why he is wearing the lion pelt [in] *Coming to America* (movie) is your reference.
Ref.; *I Am Raymond Washington* – who rebuilt the Crypts who were the old Sky-walkers.
Ref.; *FBI Informant Darthard Perry* – Black Panther Party infiltrate
Bloods (Red House) --   **Crypts** (Blue House) (prev. Sky-Walkers)

40. *Co-Intel-Pro* is an effort within the FBI to "stop the rise of any Black Messiah that would electrify the hearts and minds of the people." They went inside of our community and neutralized [and killed] any potential leaders, e.g. Huey Lewis of the Black Panthers, Malcolm X, MLK, etc. Spies from inside

the community included teachers, youth authorities, welfare, child protection services, VISTA, etc., to sabotage any effort for freedom. [There was the] assassination of Emmett Till, aka. Little Horn. They caught him whistling Dixie which is the war sign for raising the warriors in the south. It's a very specific whistle that the Chiefs do that they know it's time to go to war.

> [***C.I.A Counterintelligence Program (Cointelpro)***
> Briefing on its five major objectives:
> 1. Prevent the COALITION of militant Black Nationalist groups.
> 2. Prevent the RISE OF A "MESSIAH" who could unify, and electrify the militant Black Nationalist movement.
> 3. Prevent VIOLENCE on the part of Black Nationalist groups.
> 4. Prevent militant Black Nationalist groups and leaders from gaining RESPECTABILITY by discrediting them.
> 5. A final goal should be to prevent the long-range GROWTH of militant black organizations.]

41. The Moor Zionist Jew publication is *Morals and Dogma*, written by Albert Pike who is also Adam Whiteshaw; Albert Pike is the pen-name, and [he is] George Washington in the photograph. The Protocols goes back to Adam Whiteshaw of the Levarian Illuminati. The symbol on The Protocols is the same symbol on the statue in the square in Europe – the double headed eagle. This is the symbol of the *Mason 32 Degree Scottish Rites*. Remember, Noble Drew Ali said that they came in hostile off the left bump. The art form in the square is of the Moor eating the babies – he looks pale [face here]. The pale ones are called Khazarians, but they are siblings on the Bloodline. The statue is a marker of the grievances of why they [Moors] got kicked out of Europe. The Khazarians were called tawny Moors. They were the offspring of the Moorish Priests and of the Temple Priestess

slaves. They did not get a Birth Rite by Enlil. He never honored them, so they became in charge of the finances; the banking system in international commerce according to a doctrine called the *Universal Commerce Codes (UCC) – The Law of Nations*. This book is more sacred than the Bible. It is Babylonian money magic on a world level. When they say nationality is the order of the day, you have to be a citizen.

42. A Moor clerk went behind the back of Noble Drew Ali and added a contractual line of U.S. CITIZENSHIP to the rear of the *Moor Science Temple*(non-Zionist) identification cards. This meant that it reverted the person back into his or her [corp.] Straw-man. Whoever was the Temple Clerk was unknowingly blocking the person's sovereignty.

43. The *Canaanite Temple* was a whole separate entity from the *Moor Science Temple*. Noble Drew Ali was betrayed and arrested and beaten severely and later died. Under the Circle-7, the only thing missing was the unity key that we lacked because the invaders came to divide and conquer. Circle-7 with 4 gates- north on the bottom- south on the top, west on the left- east on the right side.

44. The Dirty Moors are *Anunnaki* – a reptilian hybrid. We look like fried chicken to them. The Dirty Moors used the pale face to block us from the institutions. The pale face was used as a cat's paw. We were to never figure out that the real enemy look like us, but they are not us. We were supposed to get so mad as to start a race war and we were to kill each other, not knowing that our real enemy was melanated – not a pale face. The pale skin was to get murdered by us in a genocidal redemption program [and the entities feed off the louche created]. That is the tool of conquest that they used [in the past]; chattel taming humans who own other humans. They didn't only use racism, they

use sexism, they use social engineering and conditioning. Social programs is called 'chattel herding.'

45. The educational system is deliberately designed to mis-educate our children and give us a false identity of self. When you suppress who you are, you embrace your ego which is responsible for all of your hatreds, your bitterness; the storage department for all of your traumas. That is why no one wants to do *shadow work. When you accuse somebody of something, then you have to look within – you will find the same. The only ones who are not supposed to be on this planet are the invaders, and they are being exposed.

> *Shadow work: breaks you out of the constraints to your power. Confronting your demons, healing your traumas; what you have been through, going through some type of Rites to heal, clear your conscious. When you clear up your own karma, you release generational curses. It is through these traumas that these generational curses resurface to live again in this time. We must overcome the traumas of the warfare that we have been under.

46. Coming to find out that it has nothing to do with skin color, because the white man is not even white. The [real] white man came over here with all of those titles; English, French, Dutch, Italian, Portuguese, Spaniard, Conquistador, Tawny, Black-a-Moor, and they all looked like us. [They brought Caucasians first as slaves]. The problem is that they don't know love. All they know is sociology, or as Bobby E. Wright would say, 'psychopathic.' The Pale faces that were loyal to them blocked us out of institutions of higher learning and financial institutions; they hired bandits to rob the family banks; Jesse James, Billy the Kid, were not pale face people but their job was to rob our banks, the family bank, so that

they could centralized the banking system. That is why they are always robbing a remote village leaving with the gold, because we didn't believe in credit.

47. [In our] towns 'Big Momma' was the banker of the town. They called her a Mayer – a female horse. It is a Matriarchal position. Those robbers were Freemasons and Knights of Templar. The trains they were robbing were delivering our stuff – native goods. Also Wyatt Earp and Bill Masterson were killing off all the buffalo and selling the skins –leaving the caucus [to rot]. They were hired by the same Dirty Moors to take out our food source. *Young Elder*; The quote was "If we kill the buffalo, we kill the Natives."

48. *Rod*: The killing of the buffalo was a Babylonian Blood-letting ritual to subjugate the women. It releases a lot of Blood pheromones from fear into the air. If you read where someone encounters an angel, and they say that they started to fear, the angel would say "fear not." That is because they [the angel] cannot stay where fear is. Women are angels in human bodies, but they do not know it yet.

49. The buffalo was traded out for a modern day food source called bovine (cows). Why? Buffalo (bison) meat has poly-unsaturated fat. Bovine has poly-saturated fat. The saturated fat turns into a white paste in the brain that looks like lard. The unsaturated fat in the brain looks like mineral oil—it's clear. So they clog the brain up [with saturated fat] so the Elders cannot remember anything because the plaque in the brain interrupts the communication between the neurological synapses.

50. On the Conjure War, they forbid us to practice Voodoo (Vodun). Vodun was our national religion. Vodun is a spiritual practice that develops the character of the individual

but the side effect is we turn into anti-bodies [protection] for the Earth. We figure out how to clean up anybody's mess that is on the planet. That is why they wanted us to stay away from the Vodun [practices]. But then they used all the practices of the Vodun against us. They use primarily three doctrines for the Conjure, and they will use any doctrine outside of the three that will work for any conjure. The three are: Babylonian money magic, Blood magic, and sex magic.

51. I need to know the doctrine of the people on the land. Once I know their doctrine then I know why they are on our land. The white supremist doctrine is predicated on the *Phineas Priesthood*. They came because someone invited them over because we could not get into any institutions. We requested of England all of their derelicts (rejects). The witch hunts started in Salem, North Carolina, [in] the Gullah-Gee Chee territory.

52. *Young Elder*: King George I was dark skin. Great Britain was ran by Moors all the way up until 1837; until they got usurped by Queen Victoria. The prisons were emptied and sent to other parts of the world like Australia and New Zealand. In 1715 they sent the prisoners to America and started forming the colonies. In 1773 they started the Revolutionary War to fight against the Dirty Moors. The British Red Coats were [or represented] the Moors.

53. *Rod*: The criminals entered the institutions to pass us the information. That is what the 'Black face' was all about; to tell us that some niggers are behind us. They were telling us that the Black-a-Moors were behind the whole program. Everything that we have been taught is reversed.
Young Elder: We have Horace Greeley and the Smithsonian Institution to thank for it. They twisted us good with the

Pocahontas and John Smith story, and the Pilgrim story. We were not mixing with white folks over here. These story characters were Natives and Etruscan Moors—not white.
[Pocahontas is Mataoka Amonute; John Rolfe is John Smith]

54. *Rod*: They [the Moors] had their own Tribes in the Appalachian Mountains – the Tribe of Scota. They were the first refugees from Scotland. When *Scota* and *Scotia* came over [here] they split. Scotia [dark skin] went north into Canada. Scota's children became the children of *Maman Brigitte'* of the Vodun in the Appalachian Mts.; red head, freckle face hicks.
Young Elder: Mataoka (Pocahontas), was a Princess of the *Powhatan Confederacy of Tribes of Algonquin Tribes* in the Tidewater region of what became Virginia that came together. Her father was the Powhatan Chief over the Confederation of Tribes; the head Chief. He would not go to England for fear of death. [*Mataoka* went to England and] returned to America with child. This is how the Dirty Moors tied into the Bloodline to become inheritors on the land. Anyone kin to John Roth could then come in and settle to our land. This is the exercise of the *Mother Rite*.

55. *Rod*: *Mataoka* (Pocahontas) was taken to England to be confirmed because they thought they had captured one of the red haired Princesses. You have one that was milky colored; Scota [*Maman Brigitte*] is a pale face Orisha. This is who they thought they had captured when they caught Mataoka, but her [Scota] signature is her red hair. It was Scota's magic that was used in Europe that caused the Moors to be kicked out. He clans were using conjure. That is what the wars of St. Patrick was about when he invade Ireland and Scotland and killed the Priests of Scota.

56. These were the twins [Scota and Scotia] out of the Twelve Daughters of Isis. [Over] all the years there are different denominations of Priestesses; there are *Eastern Stars, Sisters of Isis, Daughters of Isis, Sisters of Sekmek, Sisters of Auset, the Si Priestesses,* etc. There are different denominations with different functions.

57. Since I've been studying, [I've found that] 80 percent of those who look like us, wearing fezzes are putting the real info back out. We call them **Righteous Moors**; *C. Freeman Hill* was exposing the conjure by teaching us metaphysics; *Hakim Bey* was showing us the Tribes inside the Moors by identifying native heritage; *Taj Tarik Bey* has been teaching us civics. If you do not overstand civics, you are going to keep using their system to get us free which verified the sanction of being an imbecile, unable to administer your own affairs, therefore the Pope has got to do it for you. *[Bey; a Turkic title for a chieftain, and an honoree; traditionally applied to people with special lineage to leaders of Turkic kingdoms, emirates, sultanates, and empires in Central and South Asia, and Middle East. (Wikipedia)]*

58. As soon as someone comes out and pull their card, he [the Pope] is going to call all of their money home. Oops, they already did. Now that is in the sum of at least a trillion dollars. So why are we not seeing any residual effects of a trillion dollar hole in the global economy? Somebody is lying somewhere. Taking a trillion dollars out of the global economy is going to cause currency to either increase in value or drop the bottom out. Neither of those have taken place yet, so I believe that the bottom fell out, but we don't know it yet. They have not told the average everyday Joe. I know that the World Bank International Monetary Fund has been ceased by what they call the 'Earth Alliance.' All of the private shareholders, if they wanted their holdings when DJT

flew the flag with no stars, was a call to get your –ish. They didn't come. Their strong hold right now is still Switzerland, but the Swiss has stepped aside to let the 'Earth Alliance' eradicate ...(?). That is why Switzerland is neutral. They fund both sides.

59. [On] July 4, 2019 the [6k] contract ended [via public notice posted by Rod Hayes]. One of the Chiefs on the land had to exercise the Rites on behalf of the Organic Peoples to recover the land, take charge of purifying the water and the air. On January 6, I issued a notice to all parties to close all contracts for non-performance. If they didn't want to close the contracts for non-performance, they had to show us one Treaty that they did not violate. Well, they never made the treaties with us to begin with, so the foundation of the treaty was a fraud, so that cancels out the treaties by order of the Chiefs.

60. All of the treaties are now null and void. So now the only thing left is to go on a grassroots campaign to tell our people we got our land back. This is who it was, this is what they did, this is how they did it, and this is how we overcame it. The U.S. [American] Indigenous Rights Act of 2016 gives you the parameters by which to exercise tribal Rights. It [the Act] keeps saying 'Tribal land' this – and Tribal land that. It is ALL Tribal land! The reason that we know the treaties were not from our Elders is that it was signing over the land. In our culture you cannot sell land. You can allow someone permission to maintain the land in the capacity likened to a farm or charter a village. Sharecropping was used to steal the land in the south after the Confederacy broke up. The Gullah Gee Chee tried to institute tribal law on the land and lost the physical conflict which made us go into a Conjure War.

On June 15, 2016, after nearly 30 years of advocacy and negotiation, the Organization of American States (OAS) adopted the American Declaration on the Rights of Indigenous Peoples. [ADRIP] The OAS is a regional intergovernmental organization of 35 member countries of the Americas, including the United States.
[https://indianlaw.org>adrip>home]

On Oct. 10, 2020, the Not Invisible Act of 2019 was signed into law as the first bill in history to be introduced and passed by four U.S. congressional members enrolled in their respective federally recognized Tribes led by Secretary Deb Haaland during her time in Congress...
...The Commission's purpose is to develop recommendations through the work of six subcommittees focused on improving intergovernmental coordination and establishing best practices for state, Trial and federal law enforcement to bolster resources for survivors and victim's families, and combating the epidemic of missing persons, murder and trafficking of American Indian and Alaska Native peoples, as specified under the law. [https://www.doi.gov>not invisible-act-commission]

Also: *See the Indian Citizen Act of 1924
*See the Nationality Act of 1940
*See the 2021 Native American Voting Rights Act

61. When the conclusion of the continuity of government, when all of the business is done at *Rattan Rock, Colorado*, then the Chiefs have to give us a report. They are going to tell you everything that I am saying [now]. They may read names over an hour or two of the dirty *mfs* that think they got away, like the clerk who sold out Noble Drew Ali. The dirty grand flock will be dealt with by the Maltese when the *Chief Angel Bey*, who we know as *Jeff Ford*, gives his order to clean the house. They think we are just joking and don't know what we are talking about.

62. The only reason that you are seeing me is because the Dirty Moors couldn't seize the throne. They forgot what they did, so now the ones who know the Conjure have to do [what] we have to do – and called me to come fix it. No one thought that I would be the one to come fix it.

63. I've not seen any clinics set up to address this trauma from this generational protracted struggle. The Shaman in Africa, who have set up trauma camps for their soldiers, they have been using healing methods for thousands of years to detox and assume their soldiers back into society. Sigmund Freud was trained by African Shaman, [yet] they say he is the father of psychology. *Gustave LeBon* wrote a book called *The Crowd*, used these works prior to Freud. *Dr. Benjamin Rush*, 1746-1813, *Willie Lynch Theory* derived from the work of *Samuel A. Cartwright, Drapetomania*, 1851 on mental illness cause of enslaved Africans fleeing captivity.

64. A maxim of the Catholic Church is "If we can get their kids for the first seven years of their lives, we have them for life." The Matriarchy is to protect and educate the children first. You cannot let outsiders educate your children and think that they are not going to use it toward their advantage.
Dr. Kia: You cannot take your children to these therapists because look at what it breaks down to; The-rapist. Rod: Warrant = War Rant = a continuous declaration of war. We did not have prisons here. The first prisons were not till the 1800s; the first in Pennsylvania 1851. Everything that we did was weaponized against us. When we try to be ourselves, we get trapped into the weapons [of their] warfare.

65. The prisoner of war camps they called '*Plantations.*' They still had to come up with a way to enslave the Chiefs, so

that we wouldn't reclaim the land. That is why they converted our castles into prisons and mental institutions and state prisons. Lewis and Clark were the ones who declared the land abandoned and that Plymouth Rock was much bigger than the Hudson Bay [or Boston Harbor]. So they classified us under the *'Salvage Law'* as *'Lost at sea.'* It does not apply under 'free white persons' in law.

66. Esquire was prohibited as a Title of Nobility. The BAR Association = *British Accreditation Registry* of Barristers which was first established in Savannah, Georgia, in 1863, [previously active as early as 1790] *by King George III*. Then they moved the charter to the 'crash site' which became the BAR Association in Washington D.C. Then they started franchising Lodge Houses all over the land because the Bar Assoc. is a paternal brotherhood. That is why none of them [lawyers] have a license to practice law [here].*[Ref.; https://www.thelibertybeacon.com>bitish-accreditation]*

> [Notes: ***King George III** [born1738 –died 1820] was King of Great Britain and Ireland from October 1760 to 1820; and during the U.S. Revolutionary War.
> ***Sophia Charlotte of Mecklenburg-Strelitz, Germany** at the age of 17, married King George III of Britain. The marriage was a success and the couple had 15 children, including George IV. As Queen of Great Britain and Ireland from 1761 – 1818, she had become Britain's+ longest serving queen, serving 57 years and 70 days. Queen Sophia Charlotte was of mixed (Moorish) ancestry. Amongst as many as 23 documented locations named in honor of the queen include:
> ***Charlotte, Virginia**; the home of President Thomas Jefferson.
> ***Charlotte, North Carolina**; known as the 'Queen City' was founded in 1768.
> ***Queen Charlotte Islands**; off the northern coast of British Columbia, was named by Captain James Dixon in 1787.

(Queen's College; its' charter signed November 10, 1766 by William Franklin, the last Colonial governor of New Jersey.
   Ref.; Invisible Queen, Mixed Ancestry Revealed by Stephanie E. Myers, December 2016.
   Ref.; Britannica.]

In Massachusetts a Chief would walk into the court and take his tribal member and say "we have nothing to do with what you all are doing over here" and walk out with his tribal member. That is how Noble Drew Ali had the Moors Science Temple set up, if he had not been betrayed by a Dirty Moor [it would still stand today]. The Grand Chief had the authority to go in and pull your bond and release you from prison. So they murdered him [Noble Drew Ali].

67. The Liberian project involved taking us from over here to over there. They then taught us history in reverse. The terror beings telling us that we were from over there and taken by force.

68. The charter for the U.S.A. Inc. is a joint venture between the *Virginia Company* and *Northwest Trading Company* and the *Royal Moroccan Company*. They were going to war. They were fighting on the high seas. That which they captured over here was to be returned to the crown over in Europe. So the cease fire agreement was negotiated in Paris. That is why they built the *Eifel Tower* meaning "I Fell" in Paris, meaning the *Matriarchy*. So Paris shipped us the drag queen over here and told us it was the *Statue of Liberty* because they pass it off as the man who is the rightful heir of the Earth, when it really is [should be] a woman.

69. The French lost in New Orleans. They flipped the protectorate agreement to the English and then bailed out. The same way Spain did in the *Gullah Gee Chee War*. The English used the protectorate agreement to extend the

Salvage Law, so they sent Lewis and Clark on an expedition to survey the land. When they found that all the castles are empty, because the organics have all gone to fight in the *Gullah Gee Chee Wars*. When the natives start back home after the feather verses the fez *Conjure War*, they said that it was an industrial revolution everywhere we went because we were migrating for jobs – but no! We were going home from the war. That is when they switched us out on the *Trail of Tears*.

70. It works like this; first you have a person in the position of the victor. He can only hold onto his power as long as he makes you feel that you are part of his victory. If he tells you the truth then it will make you rebel based upon your nature. But if he tells you a false narrative and he gives you pride in that narrative, the pride in the Civil War. The 1776, the bicentennial, the red white and blue, Yankee doodle dandy, Uncle Sam; this is all painted up for somebody called a patriot. Patriot is from the Greek word *'patton'* which means father. They are trying to teach everyone to push a Patriarchal agenda. The word patriot is a sign to the people who are loyal to the land in which they live and the flag is that representation.

71. We [however] used *Totem Poles*; they use flags. On the land, the law of the land requires us to use Totem Poles to stake the land and to tell you about the land; same as the Europeans [telling their story] with the flag. We tell it in the Totem Pole. Now the narrative of us being slaves becomes a false narrative, but if you say that we are P.O.W.s (prisoners of war), now you can see the narrative the way that it is supposed to be seen. We always had farms across the country. Every Tribe had farming communities attached to

the Tribe. Those who moved to the big city [still] had a country Big Momma, and a city Big Momma.

72. The confusion comes in when they took 'Momma' off of 'Big Momma House' and they called it the 'Big House.' Then they told us that the niggers that live in the 'Big House'—the *House niggers*' was working for the pale faces that lived in the house with them. Go back and take a look at what was going on in the era socially. We were establishing communities that were not attached to anyone but us. This is called 'autonomy.' All of the communities that we established to be autonomous, they bombed them, flooded them, or burned them down. The narrative that they are painting is that we are all Americans, red white and blue, and that we conquered the Confederates who were the slaveholding rebels of the south. What they don't tell us is that the rebel flag represented what we call the *Confederation of Nations of the Iroquois and Algonquin Tribes* had nothing to do with European government that they had set up in the south. We were fighting for autonomy, and they were fighting for control. The Blood bath was taking place in Florida because that is where the *Seminole War* was taking place. They tell us all of the legends about the great lumber jacks that came over here and cleared the land. They are chopping down all of our trees.

73. All the time we are thinking it is the pale face in the Big House, but it is that nigger [the Sam L. J. character in *Jango* the movie]. That is why Sam L.J. character acted like he did in the movie. Jango was the rebel. He [Sam] asked "Why is this nigger riding into town when you all are supposed to be covering this –ish up?" The military guy told Sam to "be cool." The pale face was pretending to be the slave owner.

The pale face was not the owner of the house. He was there as an apprentice to learn how to run a farm.

74. Go back to MLK, he said they gave these people land grants. They created land grants colleges. He said at the same time that we were working as a share cropper, they were mechanizing the farm. They were sending them to us to learn how to farm the land. How can we as 'Africans' know [how] to farm American land? The narrative has to hold up under critical thinking to a certain degree. [In this case it does not].

75. They paint the false narrative because they do not want you to know that the Black Hand in the south was a nigger hand hanging from under a KKK robe.
ADL; secret relations between Blacks and Jews
JDL; the International Jew, the Satanic Jew, the Wandering Jew, *The Merchant of Venice.*
It is all telling the same thing. This is the synagogue of Satan. This is the one masquerading as Jew, but they are not the ones. First of all, they wouldn't be calling themselves Jews; they would be calling themselves 'Israelites', or 'Hebrews.' Israel is Jacob, after he stole his brother's Birth Rite. They are putting Ashkenazi's, Sephardi's, Khazarians, up as Jews and as the Tribe of Israel. The problem with that is twofold. In the whole book [of the Bible] everything happens in the Middle East.

76. They brought their –ish over here in 1492, now the ones who got the Birth Rite to the land [of America] are identifying with the characters in the book [Bible] that they [have] used to steal the [American] Birth Rite [to the land]. They are all frauds. Then they are making you defraud yourself [by calling yourselves Africans]. We [the organics] were not Jew,

Christian, or Muslim. We were the feather wearing Tribes of the Americas. We had nothing to do with the Middle East.

77. They tell us of the spirit of 1776, and as patriots we [should] solute the Tea Party [another narrative], but as Chiefs of the land, we do not solute the Boston Tea Party because that is where they crashed our land mass into their ship. Malcolm X said "we did not land on Plymouth Rock, Plymouth Rock landed on us." [This was in reference to the landing of the British *Mayflower* ship 1620 on what is today called Cape Cod, Massachusetts].

> [May is a celebration of "Our Lady the Virgin Mary" in France. It is commemorated by 'The Mays' which are huge canvas paintings that hung in the *Notre Dame Cathedral*, but survived the April 15, 2019 Cathedral fire in Paris.]

Rod; Notre Dame is where they came up with the slave narrative. The image of the slave ship is the same as the architectural design of Notre Dame Cathedral.

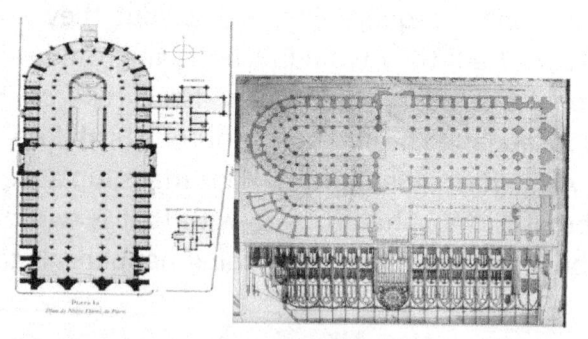

78. Notre Dame was founded 1162-1163. The Moors had introduced and established universities throughout Europe. Moors were expelled from Europe 1492 – 1611. Notre Dame means Dame of the North. The Dame of the North is Isis, the Ice Princess. The city of Paris is called *Parthenon of Isis*. France is instrumental in all of this. [There was the *1783 Treaty of Paris* between Great Britain King George III and the

64

United States which was signed after the French-American alliance defeated the British at Yorktown during the *Revolutionary War*. Following this the United States signed the *Louisiana Purchase* of 1803, purchasing from the French their so-called 'claimed' territory here in America]. *The Eifel Tower* was built 1887-1889 in Paris and is a homonym for 'I Fell.' From Paris, a matching icon was sent to America which is the 1886 *Statue of Liberty* erected in New York. These are both commemorations of the French-U.S. Alliance and friendship.

79. Following the Gullah Wars, on the way back to their homes, the organics were replaced on the Trail of Tears [with the $5 Indians] by the federal government who gave them Chieftainship by federal order. No presidency can give foreigners Rites over our land. They did it for the purpose of making treaties as if they were us. This is why the slave narrative is so necessary [to them]. The French sold the protectorate Rite in the *New Orleans Purchase*; they did NOT sell the entirety of what later became known as the *Louisiana Purchase.* They only sold the Port of New Orleans.

80. We were fighting in Florida, leaving our homes and villages within a moment's notice we headed to Florida to fend off the attackers, the Conquistadors. As we moved into Florida, Lewis and Clark moved in, seeing that the castles were empty and they declared the crash site to extend all the way to what we know as Washington State and Oregon. After seeing the western port cities, their false claim is that we abandoned the properties. But we had left caretakers behind. That's who they are having the conversations with when you read in the journals. Where the stops are is where they are talking to the Elders across the land, and the Elders

are telling them that the people of the land went to fight in the Great War.

81. The Louisiana protectorate [extends] from New Orleans northward and westward. In the Gullah War we were fighting the Conquistadors from Spain. Tribes came from the northwest and southwest, from all across the land to fight in the *Gullah War*. From the southwest were our desert Tribes. Only they knew how to survive on land so inhospitable. But they left there because they was in Florida. We did not fight the Spanish in that territory [of the southwest] because [the U.S.] had not annexed that territory yet. Nor had the U.S. annexed Texas yet.

82. By keeping up the slave narrative, they [try to] send us in the opposite direction. We came from the interior parts of the land to go fight in Florida. They called us *Seminole* because the Tribes are mixed and their narrative is "that the slaves ran away to Florida and joined with the native Tribes." That is bullshit. Go to North and South Carolina and talk to the *Gee Chee*. They will tell you that they have always been there. They don't know where the African narrative story is coming from. They don't know anything about being a Seminole because what their Ancestors told them there were *Getty Gee Chee; Gee Chee Gullah; Gullah Gee Chee; Getty Gullah Gee Chee*; they are all different branches of the same Tribe. So the slave narrative is to cover up the transfer of us darker indigenous people to the land and replace us with the *Mongols, the Huns, and the Hindus* that they had as their servants; that they brought over here. It's a control narrative; the victor is only going to tell his story to the people to make them less resistant to his tyranny. Look at what they do with the money. They send billions of dollars over seas to everybody else but do not spend any of it here. They are

sending the Ukraine all of that money and military –ish, but America does not own all of that military equipment. This is what we do know, the only military that is supposed to be over here that is not the militia of the people is the National Guard. The commander, the other branches of the military and use that as a fighting force for the bankers.

83. The [our] Army was the ground troops of what we called 'The Braves.' The Navy was the sea people. Know your people and how we moved on the land. We learn how to assess the terrain. How do the guys in Mississippi move different from the guys in the city? The trick is to give a brother his respect when you get there. Real recognizes real.

84. The slave narrative is a put together narrative so that we don't know that we were P.O.W.s – Prisoners of war. We never stopped fighting. The fight just went from physical to conjure. Fezzes verses feathers in the amnesia of self-discovery. So they tell you the slave narrative to make you hold on to the victim period. You've got to remain the victim until you heal from it. The trauma is still there; trauma of being a P.O.W. is no different than the trauma of being a slave. The only difference is the context. When the context changed, your ability to be civil to a hostile and belligerent force on the land.

85. You now wait for a leader to bring it to the attention of the people on the land to look for a solution to the problem. The solution to the problem is to step back and let it fall. But the people are in fear of breaking the norm established by the enemy, so we fight each other so that no one upsets that narrative. We are being what we call 'a law abiding citizen' [good Negro], a patriot, but being a patriot we don't know that we are being a Patriarch. We are pushing the European homosexual agenda of conquest by subjugating the males of

the species that you are trying to conquer. This is the real 'buck breaking', social castration of the men in front of everybody else, until it self-perpetuates itself within the culture. In the media: bully him until he apologizes. You don't see the ADL or the JDL coming for me no matter what I say. They will send Zuckerberg at me to block my information flow.

86. When I tell you that the Moorish Zionist Jews are holding the keys to the kingdom, and that Noble Drew Ali infiltrated them when he went in as a merchant marine and a seafarer. They thought he was one of them. This is why that part of his story is necessary for us to know how he was able to infiltrate them. He was in New Jersey when he infiltrated them. After he stepped off the dock they thought he was one of them, but they never realized that he got on the boat in South Carolina and traveled the seas learning how they navigate the seas. Then he was able to put it together and go right to where they were without them knowing who he was. What did he say? "I went and got the secrets from all of the secret societies and put them in the public domain."

87. Ask the Moors Science Temple is that true. He said that he came and established the Moorish Temple of Science as a civic organization which was to serve as a tribal structure for the Chiefs that know can use the blueprint that he laid down to have a real simple tribal structure blueprint to go and establish their own vine and fig tree. So he said "I'm going to leave these people in power long enough for you to learn how to run a government."

88. Now you have to ask yourself, maybe in the sixty's we could have run the government, but we had not gotten strong enough to see through their shenanigans. We hadn't got to a level of the *Elijah Muhammad, Noble Drew Ali,*

Marcus Garvey, W.E.B. Dubois, Frederick Douglass, Gabriel Prosser, Mary McCloud Bethune, Fannie Lou Hammer, all the Ancestors who had ambition for us to take all of what they put in the public and put it all together to build a ladder out of the hole that the mf's had pushed us in.

89. So they needed the slave narrative in order for us ... remember in the *George Washington Challenge* it said if they treated us harshly, we would not know what side of the water we originated from. The whole structure is contingent on us not being able to know that we are from this land. Because if you do not know you are from the land, you have no Rites to it. [Now that you know you are from the land], in order to know you are from the land you have to know the structure to rebuild the Tribes. The Tribal structure is necessary overstanding how to find your people.
Young Elder: The whole world is dependent on us not knowing who we are. They all benefit [off of our labor]. That is why they do not come and tell us. They benefit off our ignorance.   *Rod*:
The only way to stop them from benefiting off our ignorance is to stop being ignorant.

90. It is the Law of Use; the Law of Use is a universal law that says, if it is useful, and you have a use for it, and it is not currently in use, then you have all of the rights to use it until the owner decides that he needs to use it himself. That is the Law of Use. That includes your 'Will power' as long as you are surrendering your source of power of self to someone else [they will use it/you]. The force of 'power of self' is your Rite to establish your greatest life scenario based on what is written in your heart. But if you follow the ego, the artificial self that the social environment needs to construct to keep you tempered and under control, then you will never live

your best life. You will always be in a miserable condition because you are not having your highest expression of your best self.

91. In review of the *George Washington Challenge*, all we have to know is where we came from. We can't argue with them about the semantics of names. We can trace the etymology of Moor to its first usage. The Moors [that] Noble Drew Ali infiltrated were in New Jersey. That is the Moors Zionist Temple proper. When he came out of there, he left and went to the mid-west, Detroit and Chicago, and began to propagate. He was also an herbalist. He was also one who argued Law in Counselor Court. That is how he knew how to establish the independent jurisdiction. He got sold out. When you look on the back of the Nationalist Nationality card it says U.S. citizen. They were never supposed to be in contract with the United States [corpse]. They were supposed to be an independent sovereign body under the leadership of *Noble Drew Ali, Emeritus High Chief Cherokee Nation*, which is the cherry tree nation that George Washington chopped down. That Cherokee does not even go to a word that starts with a 'C' or 'K' or 'Q'. It is a catch term, the same way that they use the word Moor. They used 'Cherokee' to integrate the five dollar Indians with organic people who were already here. So the word 'Cherokee' and the word 'Moor' became two catch terms that came later on in the conflict with the Moors in exile from Europe and the people who were native to the land. So when they are telling the slave narrative, it becomes necessary in order to hold the people under a control narrative.

> [In a three volume handbook John Adams wrote for the convention surveying different types of governments and ideas about government...it also included the Iroquois Confederacy and other indigenous governments, which many

of the delegates knew through personal experience. "You had the Cherokee chiefs having dinner with Thomas Jefferson's father in Williamsburg, and then in the northern area of course you had this Philadelphia interaction with the Delaware and the Iroquois." Says Kirke Kicking Bird, a lawyer, member of the Kiowa Tribe and coauthor with Lynn Kicking Bird of Indians and the United States Constitution. A forgotten Legacy. (History.com)]

92. All of the Constitution that we see is a re-write of the *Iroquois Confederate Constitution* that came out of the Republican Party under the Confederacy. You will see that they all look like us. Almost all of them. Those were the organic people of the land that was being overthrown.

> *Iroquois Confederation;* (People of the Longhouse, Haudenosaunee) a six nation confederacy of upper New York state and southeastern Canada; associated with the writing of the U.S. Constitution
>
> *Algonquin* – now live in Easter Canada (escaped to) closely related to the Odawa, Potawatomi, Ojibwe, Oji-Cree, Mississaugas and Nipissing, of which form the larger Anicinape (Anishinaabeg). Algonquin call themselves Omamiwinini(wak, pl.) Native to Canada and U.S. territories.
>
> *Powhatan Confederacy* – at least 30 Algonquian speaking tribes of North America, native to the tidewater regions of Virginia, Chesapeake Bay, and Southern Maryland.
>
> [Britannica Encyclopedia]

93. We are trying to reclaim Big Momma's House and they were trying to keep it a secret that it was Big Momma's House and not a plantation. So when they finally decided to abandon Big Momma's House they created a condition of servitude called *'Sharecropping'* where they contract you. When they contract you, they own your ass. That is why the Irish and the Scots indentured that they brought over here

would just bust the place up. That is why the early European that was over here didn't like them and still don't like them. They are the red-haired step child of Europe. But they began to learn from the people of the land, and they were given a settlement in the Appalachian Mountains, and they got strangled out economically right along with us. That is why they call them po-white-trash. They use to have signs that said "No Irish, No Niggers, Your dog is welcomed."

94. They were using those institutions of Masonry, the educational institutions that they called schools and universities, all academia, became the training grounds for the work force that they had to turn into something called a 'consumer.' So they keep us under this false narrative. See *The Mis-Education of the Negro* by Carter G. Woodson. Read the back of the book cover quote:

> "When you control a man's thinking, you do not have to worry about his actions. He will find his "proper place" and will stay in it. You do not need to send him to the back door. He will go without being told. In fact, is there is no back door, he will protest until one is made for his use. His education demands it." [Dr. Carter G. Woodson]

You have to remember what they did to him. They knew he was brilliant, they brought him in the house with them, but they had a little girl around his same age and that they were good friends, so they had his nuts cut off so that he would not f_ck her.

95. *Rod*: Why do we have a Civil Rights Act going on in the 50's & 60's when they already had a Civil Rights Act from the 1800's and a whole Civil Rights Movement in the 1800's? Somebody is lying. We had a Civil Rights struggle from the 1800s before the 1950-1960 Civil Rights struggle. They keep running the same bullshit narrative in front of our face.

There was a Civil Rights Act signed in 1875 – [it was] overturned in 1883.

96. *Dr. Kia*: Speaking of the 60's, the JFK assassination really does speak to the Dirty Moors today. Because his son wanted vengeance for what they did to his father.
Rod: They had a cousin they called Little Bobby who use to hang out with someone called D.J. They use to be popular on the night scenes in the 80's in New York. D.J. was a staunch supporter of Ronald Wilson Regan.

97. You have to go back and listen to his speeches as the Governor of California verses what he did after George Bush came in. He then switched up his program. *George Bush came off the 32 degree Scottish Rite as a Skull & Bones member.* The symbol for the Skill & Bones w/322 which means 'raised off the father line.' Three = 2 bar canes or penis and testicles. Twenty two means to raise. The irony is that this is the same symbol as the flag for the Pirates of the Caribbean. The *Skull & Bones* use to be in possession of Geronimo's bones. The *Pirates* are the *Conquistadors* [Moors]. It has never been a secret to no one but us that they look like us, but they are not us. In the Book of Mormon, the children of Enlil are called the *Children of Zephany* who were cursed and who had black skin. That goes back to [when] Bobby Hemmitt [talks about] the counterfeit spirits.
* [Zephanya or Zephaniah – perhaps an Old Testament prophet]

98. They say *Marcus Garvey* went back to Africa. [The] Liberia Movement of 1797 – 1846 to a people who we never came from over there. The *Pan African* ideology, that *Marcus Garvey* put forth [was to] interact with the people from Africa on an academic level and they are going to tell us that you are not from over here. You are from over there.

Young Elder: That is what *Malcolm X* said when he went over there.

**CONFÉRENCE DE BANDUNG
18 AVRIL 1955**
« HOCINE AIT AHMED ET M'HAMED YAZID »

The first large-scale meeting of 29 Asian and African Nations, held in Indonesia

99. *Rod:* When he decided to do something about white supremacy, we finally get everybody on board. There was something called the *Bandung Conference* in the Philippines, hosted by *Ferdinand & Imelda Marcos*, that brought all of the clans from around the world to overthrow white supremacy. When Garvey talked about creating a global Clan Fraternity, this is the fruition of the establishment [of it]. Remember Noble Drew Ali and Elijah Muhammad spoke of the uniting of the east and the west. So Garvey said that we had to go make friends with our enemy's enemy. We needed to be industrious and separately set our own –ish up.

100. Every time that we set our own –ish up [in the past], what happened? *Black Wall Street* [Oklahoma], *Rosewood*, the Great Fire of Chicago, the Great Fire of Philadelphia and New York. Every time that we start to come up somewhere, we get shut down. When Garvey called for the con fraternity, he knew that we would get sold out by these Dirty Moors. So he leaves the blueprint – he was a traveling man, tying people together on a common denominator. Back to Africa was *James Delaney* forming a Pan African con fraternity. By making associations and doing business with people from Africa, we are going to run into Africans who say we are not from there. How would Garvey know that they

would tell us [that]? *Arthur Shomburg*, he was Porto Rican and a mentor to Marcus Garvey, and a pin pal to Noble Drew Ali. They use to write scholastic letters across the waters from London. He did work in America. Noble Drew Ali was a merchant and sailor and he traveled around the world on ships. While he was learning the ways of the ship, when they docked, this was the caliber of people he spent his social time with in foreign lands.

101. These guys get together and meet up, like all the conscious people in New York know where to go, the social scene for the like-minded. Here is this highly educated person form our community, *Arthur Shomburg*, a Puerto Rican, *aka. Alphonso*. In New York they named a library after him. He had
the largest collection of literature on the historical record of our people. He would be what we call the Grand Griot. His original [collection] is not the *Shomburg Museum* and Library of today. His original [collection] is probably in one of the Masonic Halls somewhere. With the books that he had, you would have instantly known that we did not come from Africa. They mad that –ish up. That does not mean that we don't have African ancestry in us. We were trading with people from Africa long before the Moors sacked Africa or the Americas. We were already doing trade with Africa and Asians on the Pacific side of the land.

102. We were also trading with Europeans that were not part of the clan. This is how Hell's Angels came about. They were on the land with a charter from the Great Mother with permission to roam the land as nomads. They are those who were Vikings. They rescued *Scota and Scotia* when St. Patrick was looking to kill them. They brought them over here for refuge. Scota's children are the [so-called] 'trash' that set up

in the Appalachians – the red head gingers. They were one of the first European tribes to have a full tribal rights over here. Then you have Scotia whose children set up in northern Canada in Nova Scotia. Her old territory was run over by the enemy.

103. *Scota* is freckled face, pale skin, red hair; *Maman Brigette*. Her sister Scotia is an auburn red head, brown chocolate skin sister. That is who they thought *Sacagawea* was when they captured her. [Then] they said "no, she is not the one." Then they captured *Pocahontas* and took her to England, and they said "no, she is not the one either." Because they were heavily melanated with auburn hair, they thought they had captured one of the Queens, but they did not. So they [*Scota and Scotia*] continued to roam the land and escape the hordes of Moors [Enlil children] who were hunting them.

104. Once you overstand about the slave narrative and how they laid it out, once you start to unravel the story you overstand that there are key figures that are being overlooked. They you show them to the people. So, Garvey was not trying to get us to go back to Africa. He was trying to make associations with other people [outside of America] so that we could fight the enemy together. It is more powerful to fight together than to fight each other. We can't fight each other and overcome the same enemy.

105. They invaded Africa under the *Berlin Conference* [held 1888]. That is their blueprint for invasion, [divide and conquer]. It was the British that played a large part in that too – the British nobility at that time were Moors. Their strategy was [is] this; to change their names often, to change organizations often. Why is that? Because you would never think to call Adam Whiteshaw of the illuminati Albert Pike.

Then you would never tie Albert Pike to the 32 Degree Scottish Rite. That is why. Then you are really not going to take his beard off and tie him to being called George Washington, to usurp the *George Washington from Barbados*. George Washington was born in Barbados and left home to join the military when he was 17 [years old] in 1751. He left [home with] his brother, who later died of tuberculosis. He worked his way up under General *'The Bulldog'*—the one before *Churchill*; we were hiring these guys as the front police.

106. The British mercenaries, the British were Moors – *King George III* was a Moor – all the way up until *Queen Victoria* took over in 1837. That is why the royal house that you see now, is not [really] the royal house. The people you see in the palace now come from that *Queen Victoria* Bloodline that usurped the Moorish Blood line. They got the Knights of Templar to poison the whole family. They killed all of them except one who escaped to America. He changed his name several times. One was to Frederick Douglass, the other to Nat Turner. King George III's name is *George Frederick Williams*. His son was Frederick Williams. When he came over here, he had to change his name because he was on the run. [Prior to his death], King George III was sending his son over here a lot. He actually went to school over here as *Prince Frederick*. He also escorted George Washington around when he came here. George Washington had him kidnapped and sold him for two or three years till they realized who he was, then he went back to England. [Afterward] they killed his family off, so he came back over here and changed his name to *Frederick Douglass*. *Young Elder*: How is it that *Frederick Douglass* had so many [accolades] and was highly esteemed back when niggers were under such pressure?

107. Rod: First of all, *Nat Turner*, the story comes from a novel that was written in the 1800s called **Confessions of Nat Turner* which was a novel. The novel was about a [slave] insurrection on a plantation. But there is no information of a Nat Turner insurrection outside of the novel. But there is a definite record of *Denmark Vassey*. There is a definite record of *Gabriel Prosser*. There is a definite record of *Toussaint L'Ouverture*. *Harriett Tubman* [also] is a fictional character. This lady that they have been passing off as Harriett Tubman all these years is not this person's name. Nat Turner only existed in the *Confessions of Nat Turner*. There are no news articles after the fact of the insurrection.

*[Confessions of Nat Turner is a first- hand account of Turner's confessions published by a local lawyer, Thomas Ruffin Gray(1800 – unknown), in 1831.Gray was an American attorney who represented several enslaved people during the trials of Nat Turner's slave rebellion. Though he was not the attorney who represented Nat Turner, instead he interviewed him and wrote the book. (Wikipedia)]

*[A reporter's quest to review the original trial transcripts found the following facts: 1.Thomas Gray was not Turner's attorney 2. Nat Turner pleaded innocent 3. No mention in the court transcript of a confession or of Gray 4. Waller, a poor farmer, and professed eye-witness, testified at several related slave trials including Turner's with frequent inconsistencies.]

> "What I found puts everything we believe about Nat Turner and what happened in the uprising in question. It appears that sometimes history is fiction, and there is more truth in novels. We have been misled by a 180-year old lie." (Sharon Ewell Foster, August 23, 2011)

*[The Confessions of Nat Turner – A Novel is a 1967 Pulitzer Prize-winning novel by American writer William Styron, presented as a first person narrative by historical figure of Nat Turner. (Wikipedia)]

Harriett Tubman was created in order to maintain the slave narrative. The old *UndergroundRailroad* story has nothing to do with slavery, but it has everything to do with us fighting in the *Gullah Wars*. How do you think we were making all of these moves across the different parts of the land without being seen? Because we were using tunnels and caves systems like Mammoth Cave in Kentucky. We go underground, we know where they will come out. That is part of our terrain. This is why they could not catch us. We would disappear, go through those caves, and come up in a whole other state.

108. Most of these caverns were under water river beds. Over time the water re-routed to somewhere else, and we were able to use these in warfare to stay underground and have secret encampment that the invaders did not know about. When they were telling the story to each other, they created the *Harriett Tubman* narrative in order to explain to each other that we were running underground and disappearing into the earth. They said we were hiding in peoples basements as part of the narrative because they were trying to track where the cave entrances were where we were disappearing and pop up somewhere else. We have mines with trolley cars that go for miles and miles underground and come up to intersect with other mines in other parts of the country.

109. The Detroit underground salt mine goes all the way to Chicago. The mobs use to put bodies in there to dehydrate them. Some of the tunnels were turned into subways.

> *Rosewood was one of the last All Gullah cities
> *The original name of America is the *Atland*. Prior to that it was the *Utland*. (See Plato, who got the information from [Kemetic] Egyptian Priests.)
> *We use to refer to Africa as the *Afar-Inca*
> *We use to refer to the Moor-Inca over here

*Abu-Bakr II, and Mansa Musa [Rulers of the Mali Empire] came to America on ships in the 1300s. They were the richest men on earth [like Kaddafi] at the time.

*But no one has been richer than the Pharaohs. That is the difference between 'new money' and 'old money.' Old money on Earth is God money; Pharaoh Money. *People [entities] have been coming to this planet for millennia for Inter-galactic trade. America was the Great Inter-*Galactic University* for the mystic arts [with] trainees from all corners of the universe. The *Anunnaki* interrupted the training program to get the gold. This is why they created the *LuLu Amulu*.

*Extraterrestrials bring gifts of technology when they come. Military governments keep it a secret and use the technology for military usage under the reign of Enlil.

* Everything that they did was weaponized against us. They take everything that we do and weaponized it against us. They turn our parties into Blood-letting rituals.

HOW THE UNIVERSE GOT HIJACKED BY THE LESSER GODS

110. *Rich*: James Web Telescope?
Rod: Hubble and *Lucifer Lens (from Vatican) was previous to James telescope. [Produced] never before seen pics from deep space, closer to source lights. Lisa Channel, author of *The Matrix*, unveiled that the holographic universe has been corrupted at the infiltration by adverse forces.

*[LUCIFER Lens; the facts: 1. The Vatican operates a telescope in Arizona; 2. The LBT Utility Camera and Integral Field for Extragalactic Research (LUCIFER) is located at the Mount Graham International Observatory in Arizona; 3. The LBT hosts other telescopes, including the Vatican telescope.]

111. *Rich*: Originally Big Momma wanted to create a universe to discover more about self, but things went left.
Rod: All things come together for the greater good. We must salvage the uselessness that comes out of it. Secret societies called the *'Great Arc Cannon'* or the *'Great Work'* is to teach man how to become the 'perfected man', a reference to *da Vinci's 'Universal Man'*, symbolic of the mirror images of the ego to the soul. The ego is the self that society creates for you as the auto-pilot version in case you don't [or choose not to] use your free will. You will be operating on auto-pilot like an extra in the video game. Then you have to follow what is called 'the predestined path.' Before we come into his matrix, we know what is taking place before we come here. The trick was to see through the amnesia to try to remember under the harsh conditions, how we came to be here; where we are today. The inquisitive mind is going to look at the structure of creation.

112. The structure of creation is a 'torsion field.' The globe Earth is a torsion field. The solar system with the sun at the center is still another torsion field. All of the torsion fields is energy folding in on itself in the name of some stuff called 'love.' The love energy tempers the 'dark energy' of the chaos beings [who] become destructive to the society at large. They become the monsters in the video game that we are going to shoot because they are terrorizing all of the players in the game.

113. So without an opposition, you will never know how high you can attain in wisdom, because you have nothing to compare it to and test it against; which is the same as the principle for the [matrix] holograph. You have to have two fixed points that scan in motion in order to generate the holographic image. The moon (dark light satellite), and the sun are on the same rung [or rotational path], but they never collide. This is more like a dual projection system. In order to activate us into the simulator. The way I am seeing it, drawing my perception view out into outer space, it would appear that we are somewhere else, and using these avatars on earth to learn something, which goes to the ancient doctrine that earth has always been a school.

114. This is the X-man Academy for the gifted. So the dark and auric conditions that we experience is polishing the 6-6-6 carbon coal under the pressure and temperature of the oppression in order to turn the coal into its most pristine form as a crystal, known to be a diamond. It's the same thing we are doing [as we are] training in this simulator. We never know there is a game at the top of the creation of the construct, and it's called the 'mastermind game.' The mastermind game is when you are able use your psychic abilities to influence the physical world with spiritual warfare.

115. In the spiritual sense, you fight to find balance in the dark aspect of creation—the 6-6-6 carbon [in order] to generate the 9-9-9 ether in the 'as above, so below.' So you have 6-6-6 on the ground when it manifests in the human form as the melanated being. But the specific melanin that is required is in the 'reticular' formation of the brain. *Dr. Richard King* talks about it and called it the 'black dot.' It is written about as the 'Gateway' in the Bible as in "Narrow is the way." We overstanding that they are talking about a

gateway. Like right now, the image that you are sitting in is the 'Sun seat' because your head is dead center of the sun, so you come in as a Chief in full feathered regalia in order to have this conversation on the matrix, because you have to 'know' what is going on in order to break free.

116. All of this is part of the 'Game of Gods'; the mastermind fifth dimensional chess game. The goal is for us to learn the rules of the game as they are scattered out in the physical world, and the different rules of the elements that make up the structure of the world. Like in a society, monopoly tells you about the banking system. So learn the rules to monopoly, then you can overstand how the banking system is monopolizing.

117. But, you must also learn to read the words as 'anagrams', as contractions, long form, short form, etymologically, colloquially, which kind of languages using the same words, and when you start matching up the frequency that it generates, it changes from you seeing a word – to a frequency over the lifetime of the word. This is a subconscious function of the mind that automatically takes place. All you have to do is your due diligence and study. As you activate different parts in the mind, you bring these things into play, as resolving the problem in the 3D world so that you can manifest from your god-self [your] best life.

118. The one who can pool the most people in pursuit of their best life to agree that we all should be able to live our best life. [We can] create a critical mass of people who rebel against the side of society who say that you have to live your life according to the dictates of the corporate fiction. A legal fiction can never generate a society that satisfies the soul of an infinite being. So it's going to create defects at a low vibrational level that can be corrected at a high vibrational

overstanding level. So when we take the mastermind game, they tell us it's a board game. So rules are spread out in the board game. Learn the board game.

119. It is told in nursery rhymes. Where ever you hear rhymes spoken, keys are given in secret in the public domain, in your face, behind your back. If you can read the music, the story can be told without people ever meeting face to face in order to relay the message across time and space. So what we are doing is monopolizing the nature of a hologram. The micro particle of it is all the same as the entire hologram itself. So when we look at the construct, we know we are coming from a light formation called *'*Metatron's Cube*' [which] is talked about as the 'Star of Light' in the *Emerald Tablets of Thoth*. We know the star of light to be a 3D geometric formation of the '*Magi David*' or the '*Shield of David.*' But that is the false part, because it is actually the '*Seal of Solomon*' and the 'five point star – pentacle. It's the '*Seal of David*' and David is the King of all Kings, and the king left his kingdom to *Solomon*, and [King]*Solomon* was the wisest of them all. And now one 'more wiser' than Solomon could come – that is what the book says.*[Metatron's cube; a sacred geometry that represents natural patterns in nature and can be used for spiritual healing and protection. (Wikipedia)]*

120. So the riddle that they gave us to unravel the mystery is tied up in the story of Solomon and his pursuit of wisdom that ties him directly into the hero's journey of the great heroes of the ages in mythologies. So while they were giving us 'his story,' our Elders [are] putting together the mythologies that held mysteries that concealed 'my [our] story.' My story is the rules of engagement in order to reclaim the kingdom for the righteous and to remove the imposters from the land. And so, when you follow the

blueprint that teaches you growth and development, you start to realize that you can conquer your vices. When you conquer your vices you have developed to a level of self-discipline beyond the reaches of the self because you did the self-work; the battle with the dark side of self; the chaotic-self that we need to temper with the 'golden harp' in order to make it shine in a righteous formation in order to guide others. That is why I say a "to not hide your candle under the wicker basket, but let your light shine so that the world can see it."

121. In other words, you have to tell what you know in order to benefit the most people. So the rules that develop in the board game, and the meaning of the words and expressions, and how to read the art in the community which become the graffiti on the wall. The graffiti in the book, he said "I was reading the writings from the wall." The graffiti tells me where the tribes identified from and how I can recognize them on the land. They call it 'tagging' – the tagging is the writing on the wall in the symbolisms that tell us which tribe is in which part of the land, because we didn't fly flags. We use to rock totem poles that gave the same information that the tribes give off today in the graffiti that they call the tags. The tags identify the corrections across the land and who is relating to whom, and who belongs where at the end of the age.

122. So it all tells itself, so you don't have to tell the story, you can just read it from the script that is written in creation, or that we say is written in the hieroglyphs of the *Medu Neter*. The *Medu Neter* is the words of the gods; the words of the *Neter*. The *Neter* spoke things into fruition which means they gave the weight and density to the words that empowered the throat chakra to exercise the exceptional

insight as *Karenga* wrote *'The Who See It'* authorative utterances; exceptional insight which allow the people to see deeper into themselves in order to find their way to freedom from the bondage of an artificial system masquerading as a government.

123. *Rich*: What were we doing? What was our purpose as primordial beings prior to creation?
Rod: When we talked about creation, we talked about the 3D scenario and the sudden emergence of physical matter into existence so that people may exist as a physical being. What we a looking at is a grand design [in which] you have to be outside of the creation if you are the Creator. But in this case, the creation takes place within the self. Remember the torsion fields are cycles within cycles, folding in upon themselves. We are torsion fields like the apple in the hologram, we are just a part of the whole, so before creation, we were outside of the hologram, we were pure consciousness; [we were] what you call a 'whole light being.' In modern time they call it 'spirit being.' The whole light being is that part of self that is projected into the physical form that animates you as your body goes through the process of metabolism; the burning in the breath. So you always have to inhale oxygen in order to exhale the carbon as it is consumed. There is an energy exchange taking place at every level, because the same process of energy conversion that the human body goes through, the atom itself goes through. If you draw outward and look at the universe, it [too] goes through the same process.

124. So when we examine the self, we look at what w are made of at the simplest level. At the simplest level we are mad of crystalline amino acids in a double helix with a sizable portion that is inactive called 'junk DNA.' We overstand that the unveiled matrix is the matrix in the mitochondria, which

is the powerhouse of the cell. It becomes a step-down capacitor when you condense stardust into a human body in order to not cause spontaneous combustion, because too much light will burn you from the inside out if you can't control it. So the conditions in a person's life is according to their temperament as the temperance card in the deck of Tarot (the ego), so that it could be purified to facilitate the full embodying of the higher light body into the physical form without the chaotic resistance of the carbon based ego.

125. Once the whole light being becomes conscious in the physical body, [then] you have awareness. So the scientists explain that they are using physics and metaphysics to teach the same thing. When you look into the human training process, everything feels of learning. When you get to a certain level, you end up into some form of metaphysics, quantum physics, or mysticism, or something of that sort which we call the 'occult.' The occult is the thing that the average lay person would never have the time to properly consume to activate those faculties of consciousness that is at rest within that person. Because the hum drum of day to day life is the distraction so that someone else can harvest their energy.

126. It is like hijacking another person's avatar in a video game. You are making their avatar do what you want them to do. The only way to remedy this is, what Bobby Hemmitt says of the Spirit Artificial in one of his lectures, "that this counterfeit spirit is still on the Earth but it was here long before what they call 'white people,'" and he said "Let me tell you something else, which was a shocker for me, he said that these folks look just like us, and half of them are still in Africa still to this day, doing that destructive conjure work in order

to seal the blessings of the righteous and subjugate them in order to hijack their avatars."

127. In computer terms, they put in a hard drive that holds a series of binary codes that clears out the bugs in a computer; they call it virus protection. This involves the old souls who overstand how the system works from its creation because the old souls were there from the earliest creation. This takes us to the *H.P. Lovecraft, Necronomicon*. The story is told as a fiction, but it's actually the ancient conjure, and it's actually a living *sigil packet of how to activate and use it. The same as you using an app on your [smart] phone, except you use a spiritual app in order to have a function in the physical realm from the spiritual realm that you already supposed to be tapped into.*[sigil; and inscribed or painted symbol considered to have magical power.]*

128. So they scattered the pieces around. My job was to find the scattered pieces and bring them all together. People came from far and wide to give me little pieces to the puzzle. I had to keep track of all the pieces in order to put it all together. So my Mother pre-loaded me by having me do puzzles when I was little. She always wanted me to do puzzles with her.

129. *Rich*: About Big Momma, Enki, Enlil, the Anunnaki, these lesser gods; Since we all came from this infinite intelligence, where did they all get their envy and jealousy from; these traits. If a piece of the hologram represents the whole of the hologram and we are all a piece of the whole, where did the inferiority complex come from?
Rod: The same thing is asked in the *Second Genesis* game. *Mike Tyson* is Iron-head and he is the hardest character in the game to beat. So you asking that question is like asking why Iron-head is the hardest character to beat. It's the same

question value. And the reason is because it's programmed that way. There is no other reason, because if we are living in a holographic simulator, we are living in a program. If we are living in a program, we have got to continuously upgrade the software in order for the program to remain current. It's the same with the computer as with the human mind. Our human mind is reduced to lesser thinking as basic gossip in order to keep us from thinking about more complex questions. They make you think that you are wrong if you ask questions that go against the standard or the norm.

130. *Rich*: How long will Big Momma allow this program to go on? We go through these cycles of the *Age of Pisces*, now the *Age of Aquarius*, civilizations rise and falls. Does this program go on for infinity, or does it eventually end, according to ancient texts?
Rod: It's a training simulation. When you go to the *Laws ofMaat*, you know that the whole goal is to find the balance. What happens to a star when it loses its balance in real life? According to our overstanding of astrology it goes 'super nova.' It can no longer hold onto its own energy. In the human form, we learn how to control our energy in an accelerating learning program by going through a couple of lifetimes of refining the balancing mechanisms. From different angles that is being influenced by different angels. They are teaching you to control your light body matrix and once you do that you become your won 'neutron star' in the galaxy and you become the god in that galaxy/universe. You are creating, and then [you] do it all over again to determine how to refine the balancing of the overall universe in the end.

131. So when we look at the polarization of outer space, we are looking at something called the 'red shift' and the 'blue shift.' One is drawing things ever closer to the center,

another is pulling everything to its furthest outer reaches. They call it the red shift, and blue shift. It's taking place simultaneously in the same matrix. This creates the two opposing forces. You need two opposing fixed points in order to establish the basis for making the hologram. They have to be able to scan longitude to latitude and from prime meridian to prime meridian like an x-ray. Then you look at it externally from outside of the creation in order to know how you should perceive your inner world by looking inward then looking back out. It is a comparative analysis of your development of your own personal soul so that you can purify your ego and become a graduate from high school and going to university for higher education. In the meantime, you have a period between the two where you enjoy your graduation gifts before you go to university; have your graduation party, hangout with your family six months to a year, then go off to university. When you awaken in the matrix, you are now graduated.

132. It is the same way when you wake up from consciousness levels. You graduate, then you have a ceremony; a coming out; a sweet sixteen, she has passed two cycles of life. Then she is evaluated by the elders to see that she is functionally fit to present to society and once approved, has a ceremony and is celebrated. Now she goes into the cycle that requires greater accountability and awareness of herself.

133. They have erased part of the training methods out of the equations so that they don't have the same family building qualities that they had in times past. We have to restore all those things back by putting everything back into its proper position because you are shifting the matrix from

the microcosm and its trickling back up to the macrocosm and balance the two out.

134. *Rich*: How long has Black people been on Earth?
Rod: Ever since Earth has been here. It depends on what times it was because it hasn't always been Earth. At one time it was the great water planet called *Tiamat*. When the Astor Belt was knocked from it, it took a lot of the water from the planet that went out from what we call the South Pole. The ice shelf is not an ice wall. It's a shelf and there is a civilization under it that hen the calamity came, drew the water over the civilization and flash froze them. So these are the people that Adolph Hitler found during WWII through going into the archives in Tibet. In Tibet they have archives that if he was able to reach certain levels of adept overstanding they are obligated by law to reveal that universal secret. When he was coming through the *Thule Society*, he was looking for the key to where the ancients were still present on earth because their energy signature never left. When we figure that out, like doing a rescue in the video game of the ancient ones.
[Thule Society; a German occultist and nationalist group founded after WWI, named after a mythical Greek legend, was later reorganized by Hitler into a Socialist Workers Party. (Wikipedia)]

135. Now, we did not always look physically the same. And we were not always brown. We use to be shades of blue and green because we were surviving off mono-atomic platinum group metals, which changed the conversion in the carbon. The conversion of the carbon is based on iron now, as opposed to magnesium. So it's an iron fusion in the metabolic rate of the energy conversion. Where we use to be more like chlorophyll, our skin was varying shades of green and blue.

136. According to the mono-atomic element that was most prevalent or most active in the system. So they were putting the super computer into its most optimal function. We use to materialize at will into the material form. That is why you cannot find us in a lot of the fossil records. We did not have death. Death is a construct of the 3D by the chaos beings that came in as the rogue element. We would call them the 'problem child' in the school. Everywhere they go, they would start –ish with all of the good kids, so now the good kids can't get a decent education because they are getting bullied by the problem kids.

137. The *Law of Nature* says to adapt. That means that we don't have to like it, but we have to learn from it. That is how we get the imposters out. When we say getting the imposters out, we are saying getting all of the problem children that are corrupting the system. So if we were playing a video game, having fun and your big uncle comes in and starts attacking your character on the game so that you can never win.

138. *Rich*: Whenever we talk about these entities, I always hear *Hitler's* name come up concerning aliens or extraterrestrials or whatever you want to call them. Why is that?
Rod: Have you ever heard of *Dwight D. Eisenhower* of the Galactic Council: Have you ever heard of *Vatican Thor*, the *Venusian* that means he was from Venus, lived 3.5 years in the White House with the Eisenhower Administration as an advisor. During the Eisenhower Administration is where the Galactic Council intervened and created the military industrial complex in order to establish the *Leviathan Force*. The American military has an operation Leviathan Force that is the blueprint for the *Galactic Council* to reclaim the world

from the tyranny of the *Deep State* that was controlled by the *Archons*. The *Queen of *Archons* would dwell in the basement of De Vatican and give her edicts to the Pope. The *Archons* are the secret rulers and are the ones pulling the strings behind the scenes. We have to read all of the symbolisms to realize what they are doing.

*[*Archon*; each of the nine chief magistrates in ancient Athens.]

139. The orders come in reverse down; involves the monetary system, political system which is a game; game of public checkers played to distract the public from the man behind the curtain. If people were to see the man behind the curtain, they were rather rebel because he would turn out to be a computer and its artificial intelligence, which takes us back to the video game aspects. We are in the simulator and our avatars are taking everything too personal in order to wake up in the matrix. My dumb ass too both the red and the blue pill so that I am wide awake in the matrix trying to tell you how this matrix works. In politics the way that they put things into the public domain. Their orders and rules are under the pretense that the people are making up the orders and the rules as means of applying legitimacy by the paper work. Our people are not asking the simplest question possible about our current circumstances and condition, and we don't overstand why they are not asking.

140. Before 1492 we did not have the prisons over here. The first prisons over here were built in Philadelphia in the 1800s, so they are not even 200 years old. Before the prisons [were made] over here, what were we doing to keep up from reading prisons? The people from the land know how to respect each other's boundaries and live in harmony. But those that are not from the land, cause mischief and Bloodshed on the land, hoping that they can confuse the

heirs and claim it as abandoned land off of the enemy domain at the close of the Age because we failed to do our part. So the application of higher law was required to override the onslaught of legal fiction called the corporation or the nation. If you are looking at how the matrix plays itself out, it's telescoped on itself in cycles. This conversation has interrupted the cycle of so many people, it has allowed them to actually see the fabric of the story that is being told. That's 'grid talk.' You have to be able to use the stories to strike the proper vibrations in order to awaken their own memory so they don't require you information they require the self-awakening. This is us coming into that balance that's required to operate in the matrix without being victims as an extra in the video game.

(Ref.: *Breaking Open the Head* by Daniel Pinchbeck; *Psychic journey into the head of contemporary Shamanism.*)

141. In our culture, we did *Ayahuasca* ceremonies [using] toad stools, venom of the toad. The Afar Inca used *Ibogaine* ceremony and *Silio Cycle* use with *THC*. All organic tribes consumed cannabis. That is why cannabis was banned because the ability for us to communicate psychically is increased one thousand fold. So, it goes back to the history of the assassin. The word assassin, if you do the etymology, comes from a Persian word Hashashin. Hashashin is those who is high on the hash made from the marijuana plant by condensing the chemicals in it to a higher concentration. The Indo-cannabinoid system is your aura field or your spirit body. We use to use the THC as a means to strengthen the auric field in order to give us a more spiritual control if we are gifted. If you have the spiritual gift and have not learned how to control it, you can inadvertently cause problems for other people without knowing it. Because you can interfere with their energy input/output cycles. We are always passing

psychic messages but only a few of us are tuned in to the psychic channel to a heightened degree to catch it.

142. The receiver of the psychic message does not come in through the brain. They come in through the heart as a telepathic message, then the chakra shoots the question through your crown chakra to Prime Creator. When Prime Creator answers, it comes in through what we call the 'download.' On the right side of your head you have a part of the brain called the *Interior Gyros* and it's known to be activated when spiritual people are receiving spiritual messages. Our elders knew this and they encoded it in the architecture, so if we lose track of the oral tradition, we don't have to rely on what was written on paper. They wrote on the paper to give us the appearance of legitimacy. Anybody can be the leader as long as they look the part. But when the real leader comes, all the rest have to take a back seat because the leader in our culture is the one who knows the way.

REINCARNATION AND THE AFTERLIFE

143. We as humans walk around on Earth, but the gods inhabit the bodies in order to have a human experience. Earth is a Cosmic University. This chapter that we are going through is called 'misery.' All of our pain and suffering has a side effect on the energy system. It's like a video game. The longer we endure the misery, the more pre-karma we build up. The strongest of the strongest were ate the bottom, but sooner or later has to rise [back] up to the top. The strongest has to be on the bottom to hold it up until it is ready to be changed over. The strong has to take the lead. It is a system. The secret societies do their rituals to harness the energy of the system. By having you contribute your psychic energy to the egregores they create, you give them permission to

control you. These egregores is expressed to us in the 3D world as contracts; figments of the imagination. How is a piece of paper going to tell you who are? The egregore of the Birth certificate validates that this is you, but what if you got switched at Birth? You still are going to have the same Birth certificate and that name. Because you get switched at Birth, the DNA is not going to match. All this is about Blood Rites. The system is played according to the ones who rise up in the families with the Blood and the Rite to exercise their jurisdiction. It's a self- realization process by learning who you are without someone having to tell you, without a DNA test.

144. Just from the perception that you have been taught through your family lineage. Then you use that as a first frame of reference to see the world. My Momma made it clear to me from a little bitty boy that we were not from Africa. She told me about my Birth Rites. I don't need no one to tell me that. My Momma educated me on our tribal Rites. So, when we came into this reality, it is the rules to the game, but no one tells you the rules. You have to learn them by trial and by error because the pain and struggle builds the character to be able to endure to the end. It is the manipulation of energy that is tied into the reincarnation cycles. Most people having a time of their life experiencing misery on Earth. They may come from a planet that never had anything like it...

145. Emotional energy is a side effect of the mitochondria because it is the feminine transfer of energy in high volume into the DNA. All of the energy comes through the mitochondria in the cell. The mitochondria is the power house of the cell. The right brain possesses the second heart or the second brain as a heart. You think with your brain and

your heart. You have to match them; intelligence and affection. That is how you produce wisdom. You get these two energies to flow at the same time. That is what they call 'balancing your Chi.' By balancing your chi, you cause all four chambers of the brain to beat in harmony activating both the left and right hemispheres simultaneously on the same beat. This creates a stronger and more powerful vacuum to pull the gold elixir from the coccyx tail region, all the way up the spine in order to illuminate the mind. They call it the 'christening' process and this is when you receive your consciousness. It's all part of the game of life. We go through cycles. We have been through so many cycles that it is becoming harder to come up with new ways to entertain the gods as humans.

146. *Rich*: Entities that came before Tehuti, and those who keep coming back; talk about the entity of Jesus.
Rod: Jesus is Isis in Greek. They just translate it into English as Jesus. Jesus is only 500 years old. How many years has Jesus supposed to have been here? Isis is the Great Mother, the Queen of Heaven or Ninma. The Great Mother who came with Enki. She had a place with the Prime Creator to produce a protector for the Earth. This is how the women decided to create men as protectors of women, and the women were going to be the care takers of the Earth. We were supposed to assist them and protect them as they go out and grow the herbs that heals the babies. We fight lions, bears, gorillas, and moose to protect the women who will raise the next generation. This to secure your future, so when you get done living this life, you create the terms of agreement for the next life that you incarnate in to. Like a radio, your DNA codons align to a frequency. Codons of the DNA is alkaline crystal. Crystals relays information that tunes the DNA to set the frequency in which it produces the individual, building it up cell by cell. Once you get into the

form of an adult human, you should be able to communicate with every cell in your body. But they take the knowledge from you to confuse you so that you make an error in this life that you have to pay for in the next one. These are the basic laws of energy conservation; entropy. They know how to harness the decay of the entropy on the dark side – the negative energy in order to produce positive progressive energy. Taking dark forces, using them to assist the light. In other words, buying light bulbs so the house ain't dark. It requires the entropy, a break down in the energy in order for the energy to alter its form. When the energy begins to move, it produces friction which generates light. From the darkness comes the light. That is Egyptian science; [alchemy].

147. The Egyptian [Kemetic] science comes from over here. The temple priest was our Priest of the Order of Tehuti who went to teach all the people of the world by setting up universities all around and the world according to the people and the culture of the area. The goal was to not upset the people or the culture of the land. They did exactly the opposite to us. But our culture persisted and bubbled up in the Blues and R&B. We altered the music. Then you get into Hip-Hop, which is the most powerful aspect of our culture and the most powerful vehicle to transfer information form Tribe Chief to Tribe Chief without them ever having to see each other.

148. *Rich*: Can you reincarnate into different races or genders.
Rod: I always come back as a protector. Gender or race is part of the contract people choose before they reincarnate. They may choose before they reincarnate. They may make a contract of the *'Seven Life Path'* before they earn their

university degree. You can end at any time just by waking up to who you are, you can get out of the matrix. Your 'Soul Contract' is your curriculum for the semester or lifetime.

149. I lost count of how many lives I have lived here on Earth. I don't always come into full consciousness. This time it was required to break the Conjure of which side of the water we come from. This was a voodoo conjure ritualistically done in Masonic lodges.

150. The overt paper genocide was the paper trail for us to trace back what they did to switch us out and put us off the trail of tears, and switch us out with the $5 Indians; the ones that they brought over as servants. We were not supposed to be able to read the history books to know who their mortal enemy was until the French Revolution and Spanish Inquisition, and Moor expulsion from Spain. So we are supposed to be so convinced that we are Moors; that we don't know what side of the water we are from. I'm Mississippi clay dirt. I know I am from over here. I have multiple lives of going through the Bayou of Louisiana to my Big Momma to be blessed again to come back into [another] lifetime.

151. This time I had to go see her in the inner city. I automatically knew from Birth that something was wrong. I didn't know what it was. Over the years we learn to read the language that the Elders put into the community. Then they send us from community to other communities to learn the other clans; what we call the local slang or lingo. Everybody has their way to use local languages. To flip code, you must be exposed to other tribes in order to read what's called the 'greater tribe design' that tells the other Chiefs to organize to reclaim the land. This is part of the great graduation; all of the seniors graduating to their Elder seats.

152. *Rich:* What is the difference between old souls and new souls?
Rod: Firs you must attach an ego to the soul in order to give it an identity; a personality type that is aligned to a certain frequency. Every time you come back, you can be born to a different family, but your frequency remains the same in the DNA; so only you can fit into your template. Sometimes in the merger of the DNA helix off of the RNA exchange, a strain comes up, a new piece of information to be shared that can be seen in the species.

153. Like a computer desk top that had to evolve and get smaller to compete with the laptop, species go through similar levels of upgrade. Poles from different positions in its communication with the Earth tells the Earth to tell us what to morph into next; called 'evolution of species.'

154. There is a code in the DNA. That's what's important about cracking the DNA code and the *Epigenetics* and the study of the two. Do realize that you are projected from somewhere else into this body. You identify the body with the name. The name is just a way to express; to get your attention. This is called a 'lock & trigger.' After you become programmed with your name, you take on the identity, then you begin to build an ego. Everything that somebody says about you that you accept becomes a part of your ego. That is your false self, because you never tested any of that information. You just accepted it. But when you start to know yourself, all of those things start to fade away. They call that the 'purification of the ego.'

155. The whole esoteric philosophy behind the occult and the mystic schools of thought being expressed through religion in redundant application sung over and over. The word 'religion' comes from the root 'to bind down' [a bundle

of sticks bound into a faggot—look it up]. So they perform the function, but if you never figure out what the function is, you will be seduced by it and become a slave to it. As soon as you find out the function, you can unlock the hold that it has on the psyche in order to liberate your mind. That is why you challenge your own paradigm amongst everything you believe, because you might not agree with it when you examine it.

156. *Rich:* University degrees have levels, e.g. Associate, Bachelor, Master, and PhD. Talk about the levels.

Rod: I'm the Dean of the university, so I will always be here. I have to come to the end to close out each cycle by making those who practice conjure close them out. So, I'm going to always be here. My consciousness was made to be compatible with the species that evolve to the planet in which I will always take the highest form of human, because I'm going to always come in to do some heavy lifting. That is why it becomes a masculine expression of wisdom, and wisdom will always justify her children.

157. Wisdom is *Sophia*. *Sophia* is married to Tehuti. When the two become one, it makes the *Queen Mother of Heaven and Earth – Isis*. That is how you put the Queen Mother back on her seat; by mingling the wisdom with the knowledge. It's the fusion of the psyche to be in balance. It's the same with nature. Nature is always seeking balance. That is why water is always on the go, seeking balance.

158. *Rich*: Rod as Tehuti, are you looking for *Sophia*, like Neo and Trinity, to shake the world up?

Rod: The *Queen Mother* picks the King-to-be. He can't be King until he finds the one that the *Queen Mother* picks without her telling him. She doesn't know the Queen Mother picked her, and he doesn't know the *Queen Mother* picked her. The only way that he can find her is to follow the way of wisdom and she follow the way of righteousness. Naturally the wise thing to do is to seek peace.

159. The righteous woman is the 'Peace Maker.' She wants comfort in her home, but will send one out to clean up some –ish when the time comes. You will figure it out later when it looks like it's too late, and it will come with an assignment. That is why the contender to the throne gathers the support to restore the land by following the steps of contender to the throne going about, appointing all the ones doing the work. I'm not doing this looking for nothing. I'm do this to show everybody where everything is at. When they overstand that what has taken place was voodoo. So they told us that voodoo [Vodun] was evil and to stay away from it so that we could never figure out that they were using voodoo on us.

160. Even in our music, they knew we use to send and trade messages in our music. That is why they called it 'race music.' The Blues – all codes. Rock & Roll was berthed by *Little Richard, aka; Screaming Hawk*. All is codes. *Tears of a Clown* by *Smokey Robinson, aka; High Chief Heyoka*, from the land. He is no African. He'll tell you that himself, but he is proud to be Black. Overstand, we are at war. The war is for the minds of the people. The people will have to determine who they are. The self-realization is also the activation of the new system with us being back on top. The ones who do not overstand the message is telling you who they are because they cannot digest the message, so they have to attack the messenger. We have different cross-sections of the community. The ones who know what I'm talking about know what's going on. But the ones who we call 'the conscious community' are [too] in the way more that the

church folks, and the church folks [have] been in the way for a long time.

161. Now it's these so-called conscious woke culture I have nothing to do with. I came to alert the people that I came to exercise my Blood Rite; to reclaim and redeem the Matriarchy and put the Chiefs back in power on the land. It's already being done in the continuity of the government, but they don't want to read the document because that would require them to do something – to verify something. They gave us everything back. It's in the *American Indigenous Rights Act of 2016*, but they don't know how to read the document. We just got to know how to restore the original government. We have to revert back before the advent of what we call the *United States Constitutional Government*. We have to go back to the *'Confederate Tribes Oral Constitution'* and issue the oral edicts of the Chiefs. We cannot use their system to overthrow their system, because by doing that you support their system. You must divorce yourself from the system and use the system of the Tribes that all tribes overstand and put it in the public domain.

162. We tell the stories and talk over the history. I have read thousands of books, but don't have time after every other word to give you the book [references]. Especially when I'm not doing a class where I'm pulling the receipts. At the same time, I don't have beef with anyone over that. All I'm doing is recovering our Birth Rite. Go to Africa and get your African Birth rite, then you are African American. Then you will have a leg to stand on. You need your own country with a lobbying body of congress of their own for reparations. In WWII Japan lobbied for the Japanese to get reparations and they got it. But no African country is claiming you are from there—lobbying for you to get reparations – giving you dual

citizenship, because they know that you are tied to the land [here].

163. I've been talking to Garvey's sons and they [are] all saying the same thing as I'm saying, that we are from over here. There is African in us. We have been marrying them for thousands of years. When they are telling you that, they are not making it up. That *21 And Me* DNA Blood test [for Ancestry] is for entertainment purposes. The narrative is to steer us away from the Birth Rite of the land over here. The narrative has to disassociate us from the land called America, but we were already here before Columbus came. So we have to go back to our system to before Columbus came in order to overthrow their system with our system. All of these wise legal councils cannot overstand that the 'Grandfather Claus' is in full effect. When we go from Amorite Maritime, back to the Law of the Land and the Totem Pole. We had Totem Poles. We didn't follow the law of the flag; that is Amorite jurisdiction. The law of the flag is not supposed to apply on land unless it's in the embassy.

164. *Rich:* How long has this Earth plane been in existence?
Rod: This is an illusion. To give you a time is reinforcing the illusion. It's been here ever since right now.

165. *Rich:* Are there other schools or universities in the universe?
Rod: This is the school that most beings wanted to come to. This is all holographic projections in 3D. Our consciousness is on the video game matrix. Someone is manipuloat5ing the DNA and messing with the mitochondria in order to get the message when the mitochondria sends the signal. Its computer animated – digitally enhanced. That is why we have ancient technology returning, like the healing chamber and the med bed. It's part of the hereafter in the story of the

redemption of the Earth in the Osirian [Ausarian] Drama of resurrection.

166. They tell you it's the Christ story. They're looking at it from the reflection of an original story's reflection. They don't know the actual people that existed that they tell in the innuendo story. The Isis of the day was Cleopatra and they haven't found her tomb yet. There are synchronicities in the stories. The story of Christ was written in a 21 part play by Josephus Flavius. It was to be 21 different people looking at the story of this Christ character from 21 different angles, and they each had a gospel. The gospel was the good news, a good story from each angle. Soon as you get caught in one of the angles, you can't see [your way out of] the rest of the story. It's for entertainment purposes – psychologically alluring – a hypnotic play being played out in order to seduce your mind into a paradigm that they can control. That is how you enslave the mind at the core basis of overstanding.

167. That was all part of a game called 'white supremacy', a multi-dimensional chess game. White supremacy foundation is the protocols of Zion. The script is written as morals & dogmas telling you basically how to follow the dogma. The ones who follow the morals only don't see [recognize] the story. The [way the] story is played out, isn't it interesting that America came in with George and left out with George. When Obama was President, George was still King George of America as long as he was still living. As by [becoming head of] the Senate subcommittee in 1991 in the wee hours of the morning (he was ousted by William Cooper). It was part of a security agreement to give the Illuminati or Deep State control of the government. George Bush Sr. was the king of the government, and from then on he was the one who

controlled the next several presidents until they got to Donald J., then his plan was derailed.

168. All this is still playing out—the story repeatedly running over and over again. Now what they are running is the *Kabuki Theater*, which is common in Japanese culture – East meets West – uniting African and Asia – uniting the mythologies that are repeating the same ol' drama that traces back to the *Ausarian Drama of Resurrection*, and the masters of the land know that when the Christ has come, they know who to call. They call on one of the Elders of the 'Great Family Tree;' the *Great Pharaohnic Family*; the *Ennead* schematic diagram. All members have different functions of which they must pass on the knowledge of the functions to the children in the family, so that when raised up, he/she knows how to set the structure of the family back up – the nuclear family; the head; the Great family of Tehuti; the uniting of the Tribes of the Earth. The movies of Avatar & Matrix is the same story from a different angle. The story has to be kept at the forefront till it could be figured out. We figured it out.

Schematic Table of Kemetic Beginnings
Creator 1st Aeon
The Great Mother 2nd Aeon
Set
Maat – Tehuti
AMN/AMNT - NUN/NUNUT - KU/KUKHET - HEH/HEHET
Nun - Atum
Atum – Ra
Shu   Tefnut
Geb   Nut
Set_____Nephthys | Ausar___ Auset _____RA
Anubis / Kebehut   Horus—Hathor-- Soshat

169. *Rich:* Does each soul incarnate one body at a time or can it incarnate [in] multiples?
Rod: [It] depends on the DNA structure. In order to be multiple personalities with the higher self, you must have the same DNA – 7 at a time—those are your masters. Then you have what you call look-alikes (double-gangers), [with] the same face, maybe different complexions. The facial cranial structure [and] energy of the DNA tells it how to form – attune to the same physiological frequency that produces the same form; another expression of self.

170. Multiple mental selves is being tuned into the same frequency of someone else. When you become master of your frequency, you can communicate with anyone on that frequency. Multiple voices is overlapping frequencies. You must control the 'monkey mind' to keep it from driving you into the nut house.

171. Souls look for open channels or paths of least resistance. Consciousness is more resistant because it is rooted in the ego being strong. The struggle is between your higher-self and your ego. The higher-self drives you toward your destined purpose. The ego will fight back to do everything that doesn't make sense (doing it 'your' way). You are doing it to yourself, trying not to be who you are, trying to be who the world tells you to be.

172. The higher self will rebel. Your ego, [however] is grounded in the world – the sum total of others telling you about yourself, and you believe [them]. You use that against your inner child and the inner child only wants to be parented by the higher-self. The ego will try to take over and smother the inner child and wage war against the higher-self.

173. So then you wind up in the penitentiary for five years. They were too real for the streets. That energy exchange within the self, drives you to put yourself in to circumstances. The higher-self will push you to where you ought to be and toward your purpose. Sometimes that purpose is to deliver one message to one person in a far distant place. One person can be listening to Bro. Rich, aka; Black Magic363 that changes their life forever. Now you have fulfilled your whole life mission. Then you can go on and create whatever life you want.

174. *Rich:* Where is someone like the Honorable Elijah Muhammad chilling at right now?
Rod: Elijah Muhammad has a pamphlet that's hard to find called *The Radio Head*. It's about the master's ability to be on the other side, and if a person matches his frequency enough, then they can talk to you through that person. They have to give you a clue that it's them and not that person. You have to figure it out. So, the Radio Head is the one who can master the frequency so they can tune into who they need to get the message to.

175. *Halls of Amenti* – the sacred halls; he unknown place or the concealed place. It's concealed in the psyche as a university to educate you on the reality that you exist in; to train you up as a beginner soul to a master soul so that you become the greatest self you can be.

176. *Code Talking* – Passing covert information overtly in the obvious format through the public domain from Chief to Chief so that everybody can know where everyone is. All of us didn't know what it meant, but everything is not for everybody. We don't all know the same thing.

177. You have the right to believe whatever you want to believe. That is part of being a sovereign being. If anybody tells you that you don't have a right to think and feel whatever you want, they are trying to control you with false information. If you are a god, then you overstand that all that is without is the same as all that is within. If I have any part of that which is without, then there is something on the inside that I hate. The harder I hate that thing without, the more it shows up as a psychological anomaly in the psyche and in the physical form. That is how you get cancer; psychosomatic illness because you focus on all of that hatred so strong that it caused it to resonate within the self and causes the cells to mutate because it is not supposed to push all of that negative through. Then you get pieces of the DNS flying off with no way of chelating the Blood to get it out. Because you [are] following the diet the enemy gave you and told you it was your own diet. When did we start making hot dogs, hamburgers, and ground beef? Where did that come from? Where did these cows come from? Because we had bison.

178. Because we have what we call the 'selective amnesia' about our people; because they told us we came from somewhere else and disassociated us from our people's story. All the time they never stopped bombing our villages, and they are calling it the Great Fire of this city or that city. All the time they were burning us out. All of their so called big bank robbers were robbing Big Momma's Banks. Every town had a Big Momma Bank. You had to go back and study colonial history, because it will tell you in the history book that at one time there was a different currency for each bank. Each bank's currency was a recognizable I.O.U. to the follow banks in the Confederacy. But we don't remember that because we think that we know history because we sit in on

some Black *Kumbaya bullshit.*[Kumbaya; an Afro-spiritual sung in the Gullah culture of the islands off the coast of South Carolina.]

179. I don't have a problem with Black history. I got a problem with erased history, misplaced history, re-routed, [and] re-directed history. That's where my problem is at. Because we see that this was the Masonic practice of shifting the story slightly out of context so it says what it say, but it doesn't mean what it says. This is what we are talking about when we are looking at all of these different edicts that the Catholic Church has given to slaughter us over here. But then we want to be taking on false identities that disassociate us from the land, giving the invaders the right to cease the land. They can't have it. They have already lied about all of these treaties, because we don't believe in selling the land. You can't sell your Momma.

180. *Rich:* You hear so much about how they flooded the land, like Lake Linear. Underneath the lakes are thousands and thousands of Black people.
Rod: It's not just the lakes, the sand bars of the golf courses use to have structures on it. They bombed them underwater. That is why you have a whole half of New Orleans under water; under the Gulf. Most of us don't even know that, but I remember it before it was under the Gulf.

181. There are clues to the structure of the creation itself. When you get enough clues and you look at it, things first have to make sense. Then it has to be traceable, then it has to have an optimal conclusion that comes to a grand finale'. Then the conclusion should bring all of the negativity back to balance. So then you go back and ask "where was the anomaly?" It was in the history books. Where was the plan hatched? Notre Dame. How do you know this? Because the slave ship is a perfect lay over for Notre Dame Cathedral in

Paris, France. That is where they hashed the plot. What was the plot based on? Plato's Republic. It is a democratic society. When we are looking at the Republic, what is the narrative playing out? What chapter of the Republic are we currently in? This is the chapter of the Republic when the Republic falls for the greed of the ones that were sitting in the places of power. Their greed caused it to fall because they defaulted on all of their loans. Then they tried to take out loans on the defaults. The bill always comes due. Their bill is due.

182. Their time is up. But our people are still supporting their old system instead of going back to our system. This is all energy exchange. You are talking about waking up from a fixed 3D dimensional mind state and are stubborn to the obvious changes in front of you. That slows down progress. A bunch of bulls with their feet stuck in the ground. No one can pull them to anywhere. We need a carrot stick to set those heifers moving.

183. On Dreams: Dreams serve different purposes. Some of them is to rationalize the events of the day according to your book of life. You are doing what's called a 'comparative analysis.' The nightmare is the upset in the paradigm that shows that something in the paradigm is inaccurate. So it's going to come out to stand out in your mind as a nightmare. When you find out what the boogie-man in real life is, you run the boogie-man out of the dream.

184. The first person who came to me in the *Hall of Amenti* was *Fard Muhammad*. I was in Cook County Jail and I was talking to this Brother that was a radio-head for Elijah. I was able to experience that first-hand about Elijah being as what they call a radio-producer; the one who projects the radio signal. So it was like being taught directly by Elijah through

somebody else. I has an issue with the way *Fard Muhammad* looked. If you tell me God is a Black man, he had better look like *Marcus Garvey* and do what *Marcus Garvey* did. So when he was telling me about Fard Muhammad, I'm looking to meet Marcus Garvey. He brought a copy of the Final Call with a picture of *Fard Muhammad*. He ain't even Black. So I'm looking at the picture, and I heard something say, I know what you're thinking, but I'm trying to examine this picture saying "make this make sense to me" because this ain't making sense because the original man is the original man. This is what I'm looking for: whole Negro, nappy hair, big lips—so when I see Fard, I'm not buying it.

185. So, I'm sitting in meditation, not thinking about it anymore. When I went into this trance, I was walking down this tunnel and it was going in a spiral down. On the side it looked like someone had set up little cut outs in the side of the tunnel and put a booth there. As I walked up, it was Fard Muhammad sitting in a chair. The first code [that] I picked up – I will tell you when I finish [the story]. He said "come sit down." He said "it doesn't work the way you think it works, but you will figure that out later." I asked about him being wrinkled and old looking because he is supposed to not age. He said "I could have extended my age"—this is the code—he said "I started eating three meals a day to hasten m death so that I can return back. So he was going back to source as an energy. The code was "And in the last days they will be [eating, drinking, and making merry] greedy. And this was the aging and the death of the people; greed. The greed is going to come from a place of apathy; the victim position. All of the people in the history of the world that has been in slavery and they are talking about reparations. When they can just do for self now.

186. In the past you can hold them accountable because the conditions were different. So we did all this fighting to get this far to say that we ain't going to do nothing else because we want reparations. Reparations is a trick. It's a blatant deception to draw the ones that are hereditary to the Earth apart. This is the land of Tehuti. The ones who are the first family of Tehuti are the heirs to this land. If you want to think you are from the land of Enki, go ahead, we got relatives over there. We are not mad at those people. But we still have to know where we are from in order to assert our Birth Rite in order to restore balance to the land. So you can go with the scholarly narrative that disassociates you from your Birth Rite. Then you forfeit your Birth Rite under the 'imbecile clause.' This is how the Catholic Church had us all hostage, by declaring us all imbeciles in law. That is how we ended up '3/5th Compromised Dred Scott Negros.'

187. Following the *Ausarian* (Osirian) blueprint, you are able to recover the 'Grand Father Clause' that is who Santa Clause is – the Great Claus—a time in law when the law of the land was supreme. That [is the] Oral *Iroquois Constitution* that we know by heart by the time we were elders in the community; it was written in the soul. You can't take that away from us. This is how we always rise back to the prominences no matter what happens on this land. Anything can come. We welcome every challenge, but just know when it's time for the games to end, the games have to [then] end. This is where we are at. If you go back and listen to me and Taj, he flat out tells you that I'm the 'Closer.' I came to close the books on this B.S. 'Judge M.F. Dred.' So the ones who don't overstand the receipts, go back and check that I'm telling everybody the hundred.

188. If you get in trouble with the law and they bring you in, what do they issue? They issue a warrant = War Rant = an ongoing declaration of war. Every one of us are victims to this war march of the colonizers. We cannot go to war with them because they have us out-gunned. The only thing we can do is exercise a superior Blood Rite to them by using our system to oust their system. Everybody who wants to use their system to fight their system, then wonder why they are not being successful. What are you fighting for? You have no stake in the claim. They are claiming your –ish, and you are marching to be a part of their claim to your –ish. No, we are not marching. We are going to wake the people up in waves. By the time they know who Rod Hayes is – this duck is going to be cooked-- well done – fricasseed. This –ish will not be going on much longer. For those who are out here, this season is over – it's a rap. I'm just waiting on this artificial system to fall. Our people are holding it up, begging it to stay. Let it go!

YAKUB GRAFTED BEINGS REVISITED

189. Familiarity with Yakub doctrine through Master Fard Muhammad and the Nation of Islam. Elijah said he learned that there was a big head youth playing with magnets and found that magnets attract. Yakub decided that he would make an inferior people to rule over his kingdom for six thousand years. Elijah said that the time we are in now is the end of the time of the reign of the role of Yakub grafted double. We must first trace the word Yakub which is a Hebrew word pronounced as Yakub, spelled in Hebrew using the English script; the transliteration translation of a word with intent, which is different from the topic in modern day English. References are often added in brackets to make the language coherent to an English speaking person in the

translation. Yakub biblically is Jacob, whose significance is that he was the fraternal twin to a brother named Esau. The Hebrew believe that the pale face Europeans are *Edomites*, but that is not possible. If you go back to the story of Adam and Eve; Adam's name is also Edom in Hebrew. The story is being broke up to confuse the reader. So Adam's twin brother is Jacob. Adam had two sons, Cain and Abel. They offered up offerings to the heavens. Abel's offering was acceptable as a farmer of wheat and grains. But Cain was a herder of cattle and goat; livestock. Cain's offering of meat was not good. In a fit of jealousy, Cain slew Abel. Where do we hear this same story in the historical context anywhere else before? Answer: In Ancient Kemet, when *Set* killed *Ausar* (Osiris); jealous over rulership.

190. What is *Set*? It is a 'pair.' So, if *Ausar* (Osiris) is the first *Set* is the second. *Set* became jealous of *Ausar*. You have to go back to the story of *Enlil* and *Enki*. Enki was married to several wives. *Nanita* held the title of Inana which is a secret word in the *Anunnaki* pantheon. Inana is the heir to the Earth rites. The 'I' is the Kemetic 'Eye of Horus'; Nana means 'nine.' So he is looking at the nine when he sees Mother Netchi who has the graces of somebody that the *Anunnaki* refer to in their tongue as the *'El-Eliv-El'* who is Anu himself. We already started with *Elijah Muhammad* and we are at *Enki* and *Enlil* and the Anunnaki. In the Sons of Canaan by *Malachi York*. He mentions the Canaanite who was the son of Ham who is consistent through the *Leviticus* text to be inflicted with leprosy. The clean leper is not the same as the unclean leper. The clean leper only has the loss of pigmentation of the skin and his hair turns a yellowish white according to the Leviticus text. This group has hair texture the same as Ham who settled the land of Ethiopia into the Sudan. And the *Sethians* settled in North Africa. Those from

Abraham came from Ur of the *Chaldeans*. *Ur* means fire. *Chaldean* means 'those wicked of the fire.' They commonly translate the *Chaldean* in English (if you can find someone who is willing to translate it) as 'Demon People.' In the city of Ur there was *Gehenna*, which was a giant hole in the ground that was stoked with coals smothered in sulfur to intensify the burn. Go to *Zachariah*. When he is telling you about the Anunnaki disposal of the LuLu-Abilu, he said that they would walk over a cliff into flaming embers as if they were in a trance when it was time to dispose of them.

191. This brings us to a question of 'cremation' and why they were burning them. The biblical description tells that *Gehenna* as 'weeping and gnashing of teeth.' In *Dante's, Inferno*, it gives you the modern day concept of Hell. This is a Middle Eastern/European concept of Hell and death. [It] has nothing to do with the concept of the people of Africa and Americas or India or China. The Ziggurat was the launch pad in Babel that the Earthlings built and organized by building a scaffold to Heaven; "Let us go down to strike them and divide up the languages one from another and scatter the people in all directions."

192. That is called 'divide and conquer.' If you divide the people and teach them different languages and cultures, you automatically separate them from overstanding one to another. The problem they did not contend with is that the Earth based on geography will re-organize the DNA to revert back to the culture of the land. If you vibrate on the frequency, you can tune into the Earth and the Earth will tie you to the land at the place of *'nativity.'* You hear this word in the Bible at the Birth of the Christ. You also find the word *'nativity'* in the Naturalization and Immigration laws. So what is being taught in this secret code is that the sacrificial child is

the child born as a *'Native.'* So they sacrifice the Native; the original man; the Edomite; the ones from the clay of the Earth [in order] to undermine him – because 'Yakub' (Jacob) means to 'supplant.' Supplant means to undermine. Jacob is behind the undermine because Yakub grafted 'the Devil.' Devil means' your adversary' in the end. This is where you get the Jacobites or Jacobins doctrine in the [biblical] story of Jacob stealing the Birth Rite of his brother Esau. But it is all code.

193. Devil; old Eng., Ger., from the Greek Diablo – accusers, slanderer; to act as a juror assistant or a lawyer by profession; to harass or worry. Translates to Satan, the false accuser is the one we call the devil. Devil is an attorney who makes the accusation; the District Attorney; the Prosecutor; State litigator; All of this is a drama that takes place in the house of the Devil; the Courthouse.

    Movie: *Devil's Advocate*
    Movie: *Constantine*
    Ref: *Forbidden Archeology-* about the cycles of intelligence and technology that the Earth goes through from beginning to beginning by Michael A. Cremo & Richard .L. Thomas

194. Now, Lets' go to 'Circle 7' of Noble Drew Ali, which is a derivative primarily of two books: <u>The Aquarian</u>, Gospel of Jesus Christ by Levi Dali; and <u>Unto Thee I Grant the Economy of Life.</u> In the book are ancient scrolls of historical records of the Earth.

    Ref; <u>The Cave of the Ancients</u> by T. Lobsung Rampa- going into the caves of Tibet into a secret chamber that has a living computer programmed to identify by resonance of the DNA. The screen told him about technology and how it works.

Ref; *Mahabarati, The Great Text* – concerning the *Sutras of India*, DNA and reproduction.

There are sacred places all over the world just like Tibet. Some you can enter, some you cannot or enter at your own risk of interrupting your own frequency vibration.

195. The Yakub story traces biblically to Jacob in the Bible. A group of people known as Jacobites or Yakubites in early Roman history were Etruscans of whom Constantine sent as the 'Devil's advocate.' When you ask Africa about the Osirian story, they call it 'The Holy Drama' and say it was a court case. Around the time of the first recorded dynasty, some people came here from Nibiru to expedite the mining of the gold. We are familiar with that as Nuwaubians. We know that they came for the gold, and the scientists that accompanied them... Enki was a geneticist and *Mother Ninti* was the lead nurse of the *Great Doula*. In India there was a scroll that gave the description of the genome, but it was encoded. They passed it off as a sex manual and called it the *Karma Sutra*. In the *Karma Sutra* the energy of each sex position tells you what DNA codon is being activated. They use the lewd use of sex to make people absorb the story in the culture.

196. The *Karma Sutra* is coded because only the people from the culture know that the code exists. The DNA code is known by the [Nerthus]. The *caduceus* in Greek, which is the serpents climbing the sword with the wings at the top is the 'Staff of *Tehuti*' who was expeditious in all that he did. We know him today as the Greek [*Thoth*], '*Hermes*'; *Mercury; Flash*. He carries the *caduceus* which is the symbol of today's medical associations.

*Below: [Lilu; a masculine Akkadian word for a spirit or demon. (Wikipedia)]

Now with the Devil as an attorney; Doctors too are attorneys. A doctor's job is not about health. They are legally responsible to maintain *LuLu-Abilu* and keep them in a working fashion for a minimum of sixty years. They are not allowed to have the technology that turns the 60 years into 250 years easy. Where do we find the geneticist that can tell us the longer life process? *Cynthia Kenyen* is a gerontologist from UCLA Berkley who discovered the human aging hormone and the receptor blocker. In her work she talks about the aging process that causes the cells to break down. The DAT-2 hormone receptors for insulin and IGF-1. The '*Lazarus Group*' members like Henry Kissinger, Rockefellers, is a secret society responsible for the old technology that Hitler recovered on age reversal. In the Bible it says that God will not always dwell with man. Genetically the telomere of the chromosomes was reduced to the tips only. This reduced the years [of life] to 120 years [max]. The pituitary gland produces HGH [Human growth hormone]; rDNA copies the DNA. Yakub' grafted a devil is a moot point. The end result of his purpose has been reached—to build a genetically inferior people to rule over creation.

197. Imperial conquest of ancient royal people in modern times unfolding. In the Birth scrolls of the *Doulas* there is the DNA sequencing and the matching herbs that activate that part of the DNA. In the *Sumerian Tablets* they talk about producing virus's to effect life span. They call virus 'agents.' Agents spread.

198. Every politician is a barrister, and attorney, devils. They work for Lords [lowers] who govern the land. The El's or El Shaddai are Enki's genetic program. They work to dominate and cultivate the land, tribes, families, clans and animals. Clans are nomadic; *Arabs= Muslims*; *Chaldeans = Catholics*.

Everywhere they go they sow dissension. [These] both are the same but divided by religion. Yakub's grafting process is to marry the darkest to the lightest, lightest to the lightest, till you get blond hair and blue eyes.

199. Nordics are from the *Goths* who are tall warrior like Europeans. Canaanites are short, curly hair, ex: Irish & Scots. Irish=Orisha. Greeks were the first Europeans that Inana ordered to be cleaned up. The scientists went to the Caucus Mountains and found the Greeks were living with canines [dogs]. They were imperfect beings made with sulfur instead of carbon; [this is] recorded in the *Sumerian Texts*. The Egyptian hieroglyphs say that Isis was brought a [being] from Europe, and she asked "What manner of beast is this?" The sulfur being was defective, and if they did not meet the standard [they] had to burn in the fires of *Gehenna. They do not have enough energy to make it into ascension, so they keep coming back more and more defective.

*Gehenna; abode of the damned in the afterlife in Jewish and Christian eschatology. [Britannica]

200. Remember, this is a war and competition between two Anunnaki family members; sibling rivalry. Enlil heard about the good success that Enki was having with the humans and got jealous. In the *Emerald Tablets*, Tehuti says that life is cycles within cycles. If you interrupt the pattern, then you break the cycle. The trick is to learn the lesson so that when the cycle flips, you can jump out the infinity loop when it turns around so [that] you are not caught on the wheel. In the law of the gods—galactic federation law, when you do something in the free- will- universe to oppress anyone or deprive them of their Rite of free will, you are going to be subject to the same punishment; karma; universal law. Galactic law has us in this position because of a prior

condition. So the Queen of Heaven and Earth wants to clean this mess up. Who is responsible to clean it up? The galactic law says that the custodian of the Earth is responsible to restore the Earth at the close of the Age, regardless of who did it. If it is our job to clean it up, how do you clean up the genetic defect? A deformed human made by somebody trying to play God in a laboratory? What is the remedy? Because they are going to keep coming back, and in worse condition than [their] prior condition, and wind up in the condition of a *Stephen Hawkins*. The remedy is that one drop of Anunnaki Blood cleans up the Birth defects.

201. On Blood types: The Blood type tells where you come from because you are tied to the Earth. The Blood types are altered by the frequency of the Earth. When you traverse to a different location, the frequency of the Earth changes the frequency of the DNA. Because we are organic to the land, we are tied to the Earth. So as we move across the Earth, the frequency changes. The Earth must keep you in tune with it in order for you to not fall apart like mush; a genetic soup. You must be compatible to the Earth in order to remain here, or else the Earth will start to pull you apart. They call it gravity, but it is the electro-magnetic field that puts the energy in play.

202. A torsion field gives the illusion of gravity. Gravity is the weak force, but it's the electro-magnetic field that holds [things] into position according to [how] the angles of the rays of light hit the magnetic field.

203. Geneticists are working with somebody to enforce Yakub's rules. We know that Yakub is a Black Jew because the Jews come from Jacob. The *Black Judeans* are the children of Jacob. Jacob is Yakub, the supplanter; one who comes to replace the original man. There was no police over

here before they came with their servants that they brought from *Mongoloids*, the *Huns*, and who we know today as *Hindus*. These were the nomadic tribes that warred with Rome proper. When you look at Rome and their spoils of war; [included] women and children and [the] wealth of the land [that] they conquered. So now we are all the way over in the military lane. We have to play warfare mentally to unravel who we are fighting against that is keeping us in the condition. We search documents and we find documents like the Papal Bloody Decree; [and] they make the oath in public. So then someone exposes it. If you have one drop of Blood in America, you are referred to as 'Negro.' It takes one drop of Anunnaki Blood to clean up the genetic mutation. Is that a coincidence?

204. They call America the great melting pot where races are mixed together. The ingredients being mixed together is by people known as Eugenicists. In *J.A. Rogers, Sex and Race*, they do scientific experiments on the attraction of Black men to white women. In this study they determined originally that the standard of beauty of the Black woman was so great that they could not overcome that obstacle and compel them [the Black male] to mate with a white woman. When they did the analysis, they couldn't figure out why the white woman did not find the Black man attractive. How can the one drop of Blood be gotten when they don't attract together? You must put a reverse resistor between two repulsions in order to get them to attract together. A reverse resistor inverts the current in order to systematically draw to one another. What does everyone want? Answer: What they cannot have. While we are at war with one another, they are telling Black men to stay away from white women. Governor George Wallace stood at the doors [of the University of Alabama in 1963 to prevent integration], and

was adamant that he was protecting the sanctity and purity of the white woman at all costs.

205. We overstand the dynamics of the KKK and their origin. Because they come from Barcelona, Spain, and the *Black Hand* was the *Grand Dragon* that led the hordes in uniform with cone heads across the land. Remember I told you before that they use pale faces to block the institutions to keep us out, but they got the secrets they were hiding in the lodges; the 32 *Degree Scottish Rites, Albert Pike, Adam Whitehouse, George Washington.* They tied the –ish all together in the Masonic lodge and now they use reverse psychology to draw two people together that had previously had no affinity. They told them that they could not have each other.

206. The *Eugenicist* are telling you that they are trying to get rid of the Birth defect in the European. *Dr. Frances Cres-Welsing* told them exactly what the defect was and that is stopped them from having the right to ascend. Big Momma doesn't like it though. She said "you don't throw people away like trash." All this time we were thinking that we were living as last, to be the ones that were last, that Big Momma made first. Because they did the dirt, the good had to suffer with the bad. One apple spoils the whole bunch.

207. When you get so comfortable living this lifetime after lifetime it is exhilarating having the resistance of the struggle in order to make your god form shine brighter than it ever has before. But first you have to wake up from the slumber. So the devil is in place in order to use the law, because it wasn't over here before they came. We did not have any prisons. [Because] Big Momma is smarter [and] because we did not know how to get from under the curse; they were doing the Blood-letting rituals that were making us incapable

of learning it [the secrets]. It [the rituals] kept us in a stupor; a spell of sleep.

208. Angels cannot function in a state of fear. The fear causes all of our auras to shrink in on itself. We created our own hell [by] and bowed down to something inferior to us because we failed to go within to find out who we are.

The historical piece is being put together. The genetic practices are spoken of in ancient texts. The scrolls that tell the story directly and indirectly all say the same thing, even in the Bible – "You are not getting punished for your sins, you are getting punished by you sins." This period of getting thrashed across the back has a time span that must come to an end.

209. Brazilianization is the mixing up of a genetic pool in order to clean up Birth defects from an inferior stock by the royal Blood from across the land. The South American priest was the least infiltrated and the most effective in recovering Yakub's grafted derelicts. Elijah said "In order to get rid of them is to reverse engineer them. Giving them on drop of Blood, gives them the energy to raise the sacred secretions needed to ascend. Before they could only operate on the silver liquid which is cerebral spinal fluid which is clear like water and is heavily infused with colloidal silver and gold and other essential trace minerals. Soft metals [however] that are toxic and come into the body interfere with the harmony in the system in allowing the secretions to rise. This is why they put soft metals in products used by us.

210. Saying that they do not have a soul is because of the calcification in the channel that allows the sacred secretion to rise from the base of the spine to the head. It causes them to short circuit and blow a fuse and operate only on the lower

three chakras. They cannot rise past that. One drop of Blood can clear the channel. The Eugenicists were telling the public that they were trying to keep us apart, were behind the scenes promoting inter-relationships in order to clean up the genetic defect and allow the people who did not have a right to ascend to now have a right to ascend.

211. We tolerated a lot of bullshit [while] under our oppression, but could have rose up at any time to take over, but we did not have the knowledge the whole time. The whole time [our] freedom was carried on a stick and tied to our backs. When we were chasing freedom, we did not know that we are the ones dispensing freedom across the land. [Ref; *Of Spirit and Water* by Malidoma Some'] All we have to do is remember who we are and give the order to restore the balance to the earth, air, land and water.

212. Galactic law says that anything and any organization functioning enough to give aid on the planet must be mobilized to clean up the earth, air and water. What used to be chemtrails is for clean up to now. It needs to come out of the sky and bring the foulness down with it in order to get it out of the air. When it comes out of the air, Big Momma must send the floods in order to wash it off the land to go into the underground channels and be filtered through the charcoal and the soils of the earth. So, now we see flooding in dry places. There are floods in Arizona, Mexico, and California and they don't ever get rain [as the song says]. When it does, we need to pay attention. It is the desert. The only place to find the answer is from the Orisha. Patriarchs brings draught and scars to the land. When the Matriarch comes, Oshun floods and cleanses the land and brings tranquility and sweet water behind it.

213. We need to time this to a **Jubilee year**, at the close of the Age, transferring energy from Pisces to Aquarius which is water. From evaporation to saturation. The water pitcher of the Aquarius is broken to symbolize a star meteor flying through the trajectory of the water bottle that Aquarius carries. The meteor is the return of the sweet water that Oshun who washes the toxins off the top of the Earth, sending them to the bottom of the belly of the planet to be recycled and cleansed. We must first cleanse the air. So you evaporate the water in the places where it doesn't normally rain.

214. The upper atmospheric river must change trajectory to switch where the condensation of the Earth arises. In order for this to happen, we must get off of the Shu-man resonance and set back to the *Shu-Tefnut* resonance of the golden cycle. The UV rays of the sunlight interacts with the royal families of royal Blood because the Earth-born stardust accumulation in order to give sentience to the physical body. That is the easiest way to explain Earth-born child of the stars.

215. In order to be here you have to be on a certain frequency in order to optimally functional. Anyone denied to be optimally functional, someone has to fix it. The wisest ones do not care about taking sides. They only care about being effective; to make sure that the job gets done right; cleaned up.

216. *More from Rod*:
*The occult teaches that the journey is within and is called the journey to self.
Ref: *Self Realization Fellowship*
*The self-realization is coming to the awareness of where your position is on creation and what is your value to life.

*Remorse is the inability to come to terms with the things that you did at the level that you were at.

*If you are doing the same thing at age 45 that you were doing at age 13, then you are a fool.

*"Be wise with speed because a fool at 40 is a fool indeed."

*How do you end the cycles of waste? You have the elders to teach the young about their mistakes so they do not make the same ones. Break generational curses. Teach the young to be better people. Get the rogue elements out of the community.

*Humpty Dumpty is the story of wasted potential. If he had stayed on the wall, the egg could have hatched into a eagle.

217. The average person wastes their potential. Most loved and respected gets you the highest ranking amongst the righteous. No matter what you go through in life, whether you walk on the dark side or in the light, you still have to be yourself in order to overcome your life's obstacles and become the best version of yourself. The mistakes that you mad are the ones that design your character into a certain thinking pattern in order to accomplish a certain goal in the overall grand arcana of things, in the Great Works. The Great Work is to build *Solomon's Temple* which is the soul of man. The temple is the body. Respect your temple which is overstanding what to do with your mind, body, and soul and that being the best version of yourself is the only way to elevate.

YAKUB: Part 2

218. You cannot use the 'divide and conquer' method unless there is a genetic component to it. Also, the genetics line of

descent through the Blood is how you get your rulership Rites. The wealth, money Rites, in the stela of Sumer, they all have a bag in the right hand. The left brain controls the right hand. The left brain is linear logic. Linear logic is masculine. Right brain function is abstract arts and entertainment; feminine. Eugenics is the reversal of what Enlil tried to have done behind the *Anunnaki* back (to correct the genetic flaw). Enlil means 'Lord of the Air' and 'Lord of the booming voice.' I the book [of Revelations] says "And is voice was like many waters." This is the symbol of the sky god; the thunder and lightning bolt; "knowing comes by hearing;" "In the beginning was the word;" sound.

219. *Young Elder:* Sound is from the OM-144, different octaves, with same frequently.

Rod: There is a polarity to the sound. It is the -Ang, the A-tone that brings light seen by the eyes. When the two eyes become one (third eye), the whole body becomes one.

Ref: *As a Man Thinketh*, by James Allen

The Bible says "A man thinketh in his heart." The thought was the cause of it all. So what was the word? Thoth (Tehuti). Each sound is tied to a color, number, and sound frequency. Putting the letters together to form a word gives it the power of a sigil. The words carry density and weight. *Tehuti* (the Scribe), *Mhotep and Zoser* were the masters of the word, capable of first the thought. When you are capable of the thought, you are dialing back to the first creation. Modern science calls it the big bang, but we call it the collapse because we know that torsion fields expand and contract and at the center is the black hole. We too are black holes with the torsion cycles that keep you trapped in the 3D subjugation.

The opening of the third eye is the myth of the Cyclops that is the giant that can see with the one eye. In your light body you are fifty feet tall and must fit into your 5-6 foot frame. That is why little people are so powerful. When you learn how to harness your bioluminescence; your internal light within. You become more powerful.

220. Rod on Jews: The satanic Jews who were the Conquistadors in search of a new homeland.
    Dr. John Henrik Clarke: What exactly is a Jew? There was no word 'Jew" in the ancient world. It did not come out of Africa. It wasn't Asian. It is a European word. There are people of the Hebrew faith all over the world. There are Black Hebrews, there are Brown Hebrews, there are Yellow Hebrews. How is it that a bunch of Europeans called Jew dominate the word Jew to the extent of making you think that their faith Hebrew is exclusive to them above all other people?

Jew refers to the jewels that were worn to show which Tudor family that one was loyal to. If you had the correct lapel pin, it was a free pass to go where you wanted. (See Moor family Cress and lapel pins)

BIG MOMMA ENERGY

221. In our ancient traditions, no matter which one of our cultures you go to, we have always been matriarchal and this matriarchal energy that goes through the woman is the same energy as creation energy that holds the information of every aspect of creation. We call that Big Momma energy; Prime Creator energy. We call her Big Momma based on the galactic star clock. In the Parthenon of Isis in Egypt there is a star map that has zootypes. The zootype that controls it all from the center is *Big Momma* or *Ta Urt*, or *Taweret*. In the

different cultures has a different name, but the energy is the same.

222. We see in our families, the Matriarch in the family, we call her *Big Momma* or *Madea* or *Nana*. She is pretty much the glue that always hold the family together even when they do not get along with each other. They don't give each other –ish at her house. That is the Big Momma energy you are talking about. And as above, so below, it plays out the same in the family as it plays out in the stars.

223. All of the organic cultures are big on Big Momma. In modern Indo-European culture, which we call the pale nations of Europe, Big Momma is the old *Crone witch*. The witch they call the wicked witch because she is mean. Everybody in every family know that Big Momma is mean as hell and she don't mean no harm, and she ain't going to tell you nothing wrong. But you have to put up with her sharp tongue in telling you the truth that you don't want to hear. We all have a Big Momma, but in different cultures. She is expressed according to the organic culture of the geography. In China, she is the old lady with the big came. In Asia they say she who carries a big stick carries big weight. That's Big Momma—same energy.

224. The same is in Australia. They are a Matriarchal people and they have been fighting colonialism to hold their Matriarch together. That is why you have ones who follow the old ways away from the land in the city that populate under Patriarchy. It is repulsive to the organic people of the land to masculinize and anthropomorphize the Creator as a masculine figure. The culture expresses it, and yet we fight it. This is what makes us rebel against religion or embrace religion. You either embrace it and submit or rebel against it and don't submit. These are two poles; two opposites. You

can never find your way out of the trap unless you can stand in the middle; unbiased.

HOW TO DO SHADOW WORK

225. As soon as you say somebody's skin, religion, race, geographical origin influences the way that you think. You no longer think like a god. Nothing should influence how you think about another. You should make your own decision based upon your own experience. So the Nation of Islam says the white man is not even white and he has infiltrated the Nation of Islam. So what happened? They tore it down and Farrakhan had to rebuild it. Someone said Farrakhan is fake because he has been around for forty years and hasn't done anything. My response is "don't ask what Farrakhan should have done, ask what have you done in that same amount of time." He rebuilt the tribe that Elijah Muhammad with his wife Claire had built. He restored that which had been torn down. Brought it back to the same equal or better prominence. Then he was able to have the same amount of respect across the land, and in his congregation, to meet with every gang on the street with respect. So would you say he hasn't done nothing? You sit and point your finger and criticize, accuse him of selling out, but you haven't stepped up so you haven't even been tested to sell out. You gave up before the game begins, so that you can criticize everybody else for what you didn't do. Now they sit back on the other side of the fence criticizing what another person does when they are not man or woman enough to step up and do it themselves.

226. So what did Farrakhan do? The Million Man March was sufficient enough in my mind for him to have solidified his place as a prominent figure in our community. He had every

gang there, no violence, who else has done it? On the heels of that, the Sisters took it upon themselves to have a Million Woman March that was successful, and under the leadership of Minister Farrakhan.

227. While we are struggling for the freedom and liberation of awakening the minds of our people, you criticize. You will never get free following the mentality of a slave which gets you a slave's reward. If you don't recognize your Stockholm Syndrome by identifying with the enemy by cutting down the very people who are coming to give you a hand and lift you up, but they are not doing anything because they are not doing what you think they should be doing. You don't overstand the fight that you are in from a spiritual aspect while you are trying to tell somebody else how to fight. I'm not an Al Sharpton fan, but he has done more than these finger pointing Negros.

228. Concerning *Malachi York*, they say that he touched these kids, so they are going to trace him through a verifiable strain of herpes. The problem is that Malachi York has never had herpes. He has been going to the doctors for annual visits which included full STD scans since the 70's. So [it is] supposed [that] he had herpes only long enough to give herpes to these kids and then turned around and went to prison since they have been testing them in there and he still does not have herpes. Make it make sense. You can't have it only when the victims come up, but not have it when you go to the doctors. Herpes is traceable by genetics to confirm sexual predators on a regular basis. This in of itself tells you that he was falsely accused and all of the accusers were paid a monument by the government to sell him out. That's what is always keeping us divided, conquered and subjugated. Stop speaking on what you don't know about. Read the case

files, read the rebuttal. They do not have jurisdiction of an original origin. They could have dismissed the case on jurisdiction alone, but they were determined to override the law in order to misapply the law. They had to bend the law in order to make it fit his case. They had to create the crime in order to accuse him of it. The same thing they did to Jeff Ford and Larry Hoover. They did the crime, they accused our leadership of the crime while they are in commission of the act.

229. You can't stop it because you are not out there to put the strategies into play because the ones out there don't have the leadership capabilities or else you wouldn't need Brothers to be oppressed in prison to keep the effectiveness from the community. They didn't kill Fred Hampton because of skin color alone. They killed him because of how he was able to communicate across the skin color barrier, the religion barrier, and his ability to unite people. They were more scared of that than just him because he was one of us. We must stop them from killing our leaders.

230. All of their leaders are pedophiles, Blood drinkers, and we are letting them tear our leaders down using the media that they control with [their] court systems which they use to implement marshal law on the land. They do not have proper jurisdiction to begin with. Everything outside of Washington D.C. is under Tribal Law, the law of the land, and oral tradition. So when they are imposing their written law on us, they are overstepping their jurisdiction boundaries. But we are so busy helping them to tear our leadership down, then wonder why no one steps up to help us. We are the baddest people on the planet, so busy tearing each other down that we can't help ourselves. We are following the script that the enemy follows. If we go back to our own

culture, then we won't fall for the banana in the tail pipe trick.

231. *H. Rab Brown* was falsely accused of shooting the police. The tape viewing does not appear to support this. They have us focused on reparations which is pocket change once we realize we don't need it after we get them off of the land. There is a formula for reparations and we do not match the formula. You must have a central government like the Japanese. We forfeit our government to the settler's government. We do not have a centralized leadership that can support in a lobby for reparations.

232. He [the enemy] is on the world stage cutting our leaders down. He is telling us [that] he is cutting our leaders down. He publishes it in his books. He reports it in his news and we are going along to get along. One the Iran contra scandal, how they deceived *Ricky Ross*. They entrapped him to sell drugs to the Feds. He should be vindicated by qualified immunity. We sell out our leaders by spreading gossip that adds no resolution toward the end of our condition.

233. I have studied them [the enemy]. I know that they don't match us – the ones that are organic to this land that they call America. I don't know what they want to call us, but we have not been called any of their –ish before they came. It is not part of our culture. It is repugnant to the conscious mind to accept being called *Black, Negro, or Moor*. Before 1492 we were not talking Moors or Moroccans. Noble Drew Ali is a different story. He told me to study the invaders. He said get a good Moorish education, but he made it clear that he was the Cherokee High Chief on the land and that he knows there was somebody on the land that did not belong

here to usurp the people and [to usurp] the government from the land. In International law there is always something called the 'Redemption Process' to reclaim anything that was stolen form you at the Jubilee. This is the Jubilee. We are reclaiming our land. Our people have just got to wake up to the fact.

234. When we say *'free Larry Hoover'* it is because he is the spokesperson for the Chiefs across the land. They say he was a 'gang chief.' So! They have warlords as their presidents, they have pedophiles, rapists, boy molesters as president.

235. When you hear about the Orisha, *Ogun*, and *Oshun* and you see them swinging the blades, they are the 'Openers of the Way'; the 'Clearers of the Path.' This is what they are talking about. The Chiefs on the land have the obligation to our women to restore our own prominence, to find our people on the grass roots level, and [in the] individual capacity affirm their individual rites to the land by saying "enough is enough." They have to produce Hoover because his job is the law of the land; he has to speak for the round table of all of the Chiefs across the land. The leadership is not the problem. They are all united. They are waiting for the clans to wake up; to realize we have been in a long protracted struggle for freedom.

236. *Khadijah Muhammad* is Farrakhan's wife, [and] is indigenous to the land, and right now has the most Matriarchs under her command as the *MGTGCC*, and the affiliation of the Moors Women Consulate. She automatically becomes heir to that under the Islam connection, so she gained all this by supporting her husband. Because she has the Birth Rite of the land to draw the Matriarch together.

When the Matriarchs are drawn together, the men must clear the way.

237. Which brings us up to the shadow work.' Shadow work is directly addressing those negative traits and characteristics that you don't even want to accept the fact that they are in your character. Anything that is repugnant to you and to someone else, make sure that you are not the one doing it. If you use gossip to judge a good person, you are projecting. You have not done your shadow work. You are so busy judging others you have not taken the time to do a critical analysis of yourself. The critical analysis of the self allows you to grow from a mortal to immortal self. They call it the 'Dark night of the soul' when you are doing the shadow work, because you go through all of the purging of those negative traits and clean up your family tree when you do it because while you are correcting the error in you, your good ancestors are telling the ancestor who was influencing you with that energy to stop.

238. We are still connected [to our ancestors] spiritually. They are just not here physically, but their influence resides in the code of our DNA. Where our weaknesses are is where we need to make the correction to get rid of the weaker ancestral trait in order to produce a higher ancestral projection into the future. It's a game of relay. Everybody gets the chance to work on themselves so that they can make a better way for the generations to come. That is our duty across the land. We are the Elders now. They told me to go and tell them. Farrakhan told the; Elijah told them; Noble Drew Ali told them; Martin told them – all the way back to *Denmark Massey, Prince Hall,* and *Garvey* and they still haven't listened. What makes you think they will listen to me? But they said, if you don't try, you will never know.

239. If you don't like the way the world is, you must do something to change it. Since I have brought a child into this world, I have an obligation to do something to make it better. When he grows to be the Elder, he should not be working on racism, sexism, confused gender, broken homes. He should not [have to] work on these [again]. Since I am here, I am telling us to turn back to our organic ways.

240. Demand that they produce the Chief. On the 22nd we had a *Cyber Parade*. The *Cyber Parade* was designed to interfere with algorithms of their economic system which is down to relying on the advertisement of the dollar because the market has been strangled. This is why on the 23rd the market started dropping. All this is related.

241. In the Christian world they have preachers. I'm not Christian. In the Islamic world they have Imams and Sheiks. I'm not Islamic. In the Hebrews they have *Rabbis* and *Kohen*. I'm not Hebrew. I am organic and indigenous to this land and I follow the spiritual practice of my Ancestors which is tuning ourselves into nature in order to solve the problems of humanity by offering up the insight of the Priest. The Priest, in the organic sense, is the 'Witch Doctor' or the "Wise Doctor' but he is not a medical doctor that poisons you with pills. [Rather], he [the Wise Doctor] teaches you to live in harmony with nature and use nature as your first source to take care of your ailments. By properly connecting with nature that involves how you eat, breathe, and sleep. When you are in tune with nature you can have a life for as long as you choose to be here.

242. *Rich:* How important was the Pluto return event?
Rod: Not only did the Pluto Return fall on the 22nd that also was President's Day and George Washington Birthday. All

these things are called a 'convergence' different places putting all of the pressure at a central point. We call that the opening of a portal. Its significance in numerology and in astrology and it becomes twice as significant on Earth. This is why we choose this date for the Cyber Parade to ride that energy and try to get as many of our people to overstand that this *'cointel'* operation to shut our people down is unsuccessful. It's not working anymore. We know what they have done, it's recorded as they wrote it down. *Cointel* is not a myth or conspiracy theory. It is a government confessed operation against the organic people of the land whom they do not want us to come together in unity to stand in our individual capacity.

243. Tell us where is Larry Hoover and who is this puppet named Biden, bouncing around on the land? The Chief is the one who can figure it out. So when I come and tell you the story [that] we were invaded by people called the 'Conquistadors.' They killed off the Chiefs, they slaughtered the day after Thanksgiving which was the 'Day of the Turkey' which was a harvest festival in honor of the Chiefs of the local clans. The turkey feathers in full spread represent the feathers around the head of the Chief. They don't tell you that part. Black Friday is to keep us moving around so that we don't fall asleep from the tryptophan intoxication [and] from the football game. So you have a combination of psychology, [and] sociology applied to military strategy.

244. The United States has never been bigger than the 10 square miles called Washington D.C. It has always been a private corporation doing business on Native land. We call it Big Momma Land. The physical expression of Big Momma is the daughters bringing their babies to get blessed by Big Momma. The Earth blessings is called Birth Rites. They

villainized it and called it voodoo [Vodun] and saying voodoo is evil. We fall for that because we don't know better. When you know better, you are obligated to do better. My momma told me that, so she is holding me to it. When everybody else is pointing fingers at what didn't get done, I did the dirty work, the clean-up man work. I dived out of bounds to grab the ball, slid across the field to catch the pop-fly – all the dirty work that the clean-up man does that nobody else want to do; the *Dennis Rodman* work.

245. There are no awards, no accolades; he just go home smelling like –ish. He don't complain long as he can go home and take care of his wife and kids. He show up bright and early the next morning, just like he is a jockey. He might even beat them there. The jockey gets all the shine at the Kentucky derby. They don't call the stable hand to come out and raise his hand and get thanks for cleaning up the horse – ish. But it still has to be dome.

246. This is the hard part and the hardest head gets the hardest lesson which becomes the most memorable experience. Once you know, you can't unknow. You have to experience it for yourself in order to relay a convincing story based in truth. Larry Hoover said let the fools gang bang. We need brain bangers – someone who will buckle down in the books and study the problem from the outside. Stay unidentified – a U.F.O. and fly under the radar and keep studying. Walk in the Valley of Death – the penitentiary struggle and keep studying. Then when you get out, finish your parole, working a real job, keep studying. Use everything they use to oppress us as a means of the come up. If I gave them an hour of work, I got 2 hours of study to do. They are not going to get more of my time than I am going to get.

247. They are never going to pay me what I think I am worth because they are not worth what I think I am worth. If you tell somebody the truth that they don't want to hear, you become their sworn enemy, even though you did nothing wrong. They are not mad that you told them the truth, they are mad because it comes from you and they didn't get it first [ego], and did not do the work to overstand the problem sufficient enough to do the math. They were too busy accusing everybody else for not doing nothing, while they were not doing anything themselves.

248. They call Larry Hoover a gang banger. He has more degrees than everyone in Washington D.C. None of us has taken the time to write him a letter and get his point of view. They told us that *Chief Malik Angel Bey, aka; Jeff Ford* was about to commit acts of terror on our land. They called him a domestic terrorist and then after that they blew up the Federal Bldg. in Oklahoma and blamed it on the good ol' boy Tim *McVey* and *Terry Nichols*. Then they flew two planes into the twin towers on 9-11 and told us that some Arabs from overseas had done it. Then when the FBI report came out, we come to find that it was W. Bush and Dick Chaney behind it the whole time so that they can have and excuse to kill *SodomHussein* because he put a hit on G. Bush in 1992. Look it up. It's real.

249. Then now they got oil interests on the Prescott side of the family since late 1800s – 1900s. They are also a banking family—the Prescotts. When you get to the Bushes, they finance *Bin Laden*. The *Mujahidin* was created and funded by the C.I.A. to defend Afghanistan's northern border from Russia. The C.I.A. funded the rise of Sodom Hussein after an in-house coup-de-tat. The Iranian hostage situation was staged and filmed in Nevada. In <u>Behold the Pale Horse</u>, it tells

the story of how the Bush family brings the drugs in on an oil rig so that it doesn't get searched. The oil rigs are diplomatic property and exempt from search. The Bush family has oil ties.

250. They make these connections [to bring drugs into the community] all in order to suppress us and keep us from knowing who we are. They constantly undermine our leadership. Everything that they are doing, they accuse our leadership of doing. They accuse our entertainers of everything their entertainers are doing, so that we can all look dirty. Some of us has had to go into deep cover in order to find out what is going on in our land. This has been our land for millennia. Noble Drew Ali said "Time never was when mans was not." What was he talking about? We were before their construct of time was used to trap our minds. We were roaming this land.

Below:[Quetzalcoatl; Marduk/Ra contests Ningishzidda/Thoth for the Nile control. Enki/Ptah deposes Thoth. Thoth as Quetzalcoatl creates the Mesoamerican Civilization.[Sasha Lessin, Ph.D., 2002]*
251. There is no ancient Egyptian influence on America, but there is a hundred percent American influence on Kemet. *Quetzalcoatl* is *Thoth (Tehuti).* Thoth created Kemet. *Quetzalcoatl* is from South America. Kemet back then was only a form of present-day Hollywood. That's it. We use to leave Arizona through an energy gate and walk straight to Kemet in ten seconds; it's still there down in the Arizona Mountains. When you start getting close, then you start getting interference by people in black suits wanting to know what you are doing over there. The real juice was here. Big Momma's House was here. They don't call it the 'Promise Land' for nothing and 'God's Country' for no reason. That is not by accident. The Christians want you to believe in the

Jews and the Muslims want you to believe that the Middle East is the spot. That's bullshit. There was no alphabet in the Middle East when America was in full swing. They have us believing that all of our castles are prisons because they don't want us to know that we have castles, pyramids, mounds and spiritual retreats all over the land.

252. You go on a spiritual retreat to tune into nature. You create the mound in order to harness the energy of that you form the shape of the mound. That is why some are shaped like a snake or elephant, etc. Stone Mountain was a black pyramid. The movie called it the 'dark tower.' It was a shiny black crystal shooting out from the center of the Earth. Stone Mountain is similar to that. There is also one in Alaska. These pyramids are all over the place. They all have different properties according to the energy, like different crystals [that] have different properties. The oldest pyramids grow forests on them and they call them mountains. After sitting for so long unused, they get covered with silt and dirt and vegetation springs from the dirt, like the Great Pyramid of China. Stone Mountain is surrounded by water; a mote. It is Big Momma's House and all communities have Big Momma's House at the center.

253. On music: Music is like a news report and are telling us what is going on across the land or what is vexing the community. The love songs tell you about the love in the community.

254. On the future: If we care about the future, we have to care about the children. But they should not have to solve the same problems that our parents didn't solve. They have us fighting for civil rights [not Rites], but civil rights is fighting for a part of the corp. [corpse] as a civil servant. As a civil

servant, you become a trustee in a slave company. But we didn't know it. When *Elijah* came out and told *Martin* what was going on, Martin told *Harry Belafonte* "I may have integrated my people into a burning house." Elijah wrote the book *The Fall of America*.

255. All of these things become relevant when you listen to him explaining and vexing his grievances on the NBC interview. He tells the whole story of how they displaced us from the land and mechanized the land. Picked people who didn't look like us to replace us as owners of the land. The part he didn't know is that the party that owned the big house wasn't us but they looked like us, and they used these people that they call the slave master to hide as the house nigger. That is why our people don't like house niggers. The house niggers were the Conquistadors, Black Moors.

256. They are not all sellouts. You have to overstand they are the attackers in the chess game. This is why they tell you that black & white are classifications. If you don't overstand, you can't unravel the deception. As long as you are identifying by using the paper work of your enemy to write your way into the law as a legitimate person proves that you are an imbecile in law and that you have no Rites to your inheritance of the land; [forfeited]. But when the gig is up is when you realize that a nation [U.S.] is a corporation. All nations is governed under uniform commercial code that governs all international trade. They have been trading our labor under the false pretense that they are giving us jobs. They gave us monopoly money called fiat, to replace the gold that they are not allowed to use, but they can keep us from using it too. They are not allowed to use the gold because it is not theirs. They have no Birth Rite to it. They had it under

the World Trade Center, under the White House, under tunnels, they have it [stashed] everywhere.

257. Every land had royal coffers. Europe had their own. The Moors looted it. But they created something called the *Khazarian Jew which was actually bankers from the high mountains of Russia. Now you see what is going on over there in Russia. It's a war against the *Khazarian Mafia. Biden was on the news and he said that *Putin* claims he was going into Ukraine because they were developing weapons of mass destruction. What did he bomb? He bombed Pfizer labs and J&J labs over there. Who makes the vaccines? So who is he trying to protect? Who is he trying to get rid of? He said he was trying to get rid of the *Kabul*. Who was Trump trying to get rid of? He called them the *Kabul* whom he also calls the Deep State.

[Khazar; member of a confederation of Turkic-speaking tribes in the late 6th century, from the northern Caucasus region, established a major commercial empire covering southeastern section of modern Russia. They aided the Byzantine emperor Heraclius during his reign 610-641 A.D. (Britannica)]

258. *The Deep State* are the ones who had their real meeting places deep underground in bunkers. This is so that you and I can't know what they are talking about unless you can do remote viewing. Then we are the fly on the wall. We get enough information to come through like a wrecking ball. Even the ones that don't look like us know the code. How do you become the fly on the wall? Control remote viewing. Once you use remote control viewing, you can go look for yourself.

259. I went looking for Jesus but I didn't find him. Who I did find was Cleopatra. Where is her tomb? She was running for her life. They told us that she committed suicide with an

[knife]. That's not how they kill themselves, like the model that they said jumped out of the building. That is not how women commit suicide. That's out of context. That's telling us as Chiefs on the land to look at this situation. It's not what they are telling us. It doesn't match. What did Johnny Cochran say about the glove with O.J.? "If it don't fit, you must acquit."

260. So if the story doesn't fit the narrative they are giving, we know from experience they are making the –ish up. There is a scientist they decided to throw out of a building [window] of a mental institution to say he was insane because he was revealing top secret information they did not know how he got. The problem was they couldn't explain how he unscrewed the gate that covered up the window on the inside and the outside while he was handcuffed. It didn't make sense so the people who questioned it were called quacks and conspiracy theorists...

261. None of us can pay attention to the details because we are looking at the overall description that the media paints. The media is a disinformation specialist. How do you think that a man can get off with the Turnpike defense? The narrative that the media painted is what got him off. Not that he ate a twinkie and killed people in from of the courthouse. That did not get him off. The media narrative is what got him off. This is the same with the boy walking down the street shooting people. As soon as they [the media] called the people looters, he beat the case. He [the boy] became the only competent law enforcement agent on site for a citizen's arrest in the minds of the people that the oppressor controls. When they called the people that got shot 'looters' it's the same as saying 'criminal', it's the same as saying 'attackers.' They said it was a 'mob' which means

that there was a bunch of them which automatically meant he had to defend himself, and any property they tend to that they are trying to so-call loot. Whether he was right or wrong became inconsequential to the media onslaught of the disinformation campaign.

262. When they get away with saying certain things in the media, you are done because the people are following a story line on a movie script. The story line in real life is showing you what they are doing in your face into a parody that you can't believe because they attach words like 'conspiracy theory', 'quack', 'fake information.' They say the information is not true, but they have the documents in their hand while they are saying it.

263. On Gifting: Reciprocity and gratitude offerings facilitate the reciprocity. It creates an energy circuit. If I tell them 'no' when they are asking us, then I am blocking their blessing, not mine. Accepting it with the gratitude that they gave it, it's an equal exchange and it facilitated the return to them in increments of ten. In the church they solicit the offerings which nullifies the effects to the giver, and all of the benefit ends up in the hands of the asker. You have to offer something that the people feel that you should be compensated for.

264. *Mt. Shasta* in California: It is a powerful energy vortex that is on a lay-line and is a ritual site of the old ancients. A good place to visit during one of the equinoxes (winter, spring, summer, fall) the energy is highest because that is when they held the festivals in ancient times to draw the energy there. It's been done for so long in ancient times the energy still comes through when the people interaction

keeps the energy coming. It's a perpetual cycle of energy based on ancient ceremony practice on that land.

265. There are sites all up and down the Mississippi. Those named after cities in Egypt – or that Egypt is named after, have mounds in and near proximity of time of the year. If you get with the Natives who know the time, they naturally congregate there around those times. It's just like the New Orleans, *Mardi Gras* is a part of the culture that the people of New Orleans will not give up. The *Mardi Gras* tells us so much information that the Chiefs [of the land] can get a whole report just off the parade.

266. Historical figures like *Banneker* and *Pascal Randolph* who taught the enemy our sciences and magic: The only way you can tell of whose side they are on is by what they have put into the public domain. If what they put forth is not legible or is so minuscule that you can't put their motives together, then they were not working for us nor in our favor.

267. Caribbean: How do they fit into the narrative of Natives in the U.S.? In order to be able to become a citizen of the U.S., you had to accept your straw man. Go back to your family and have a family reunion and rename everybody with no Birth certificates. Give them nick names naturally used in the custom of your land to give them new names. Do you think *Sitting Bull* was his real name? He was *Christopher Wallace*. He got the name *Sitting Bull* because he was sitting down on the job when the settlers came. He was supposes to keep them out. He didn't send the scouts out and got sacked.

268. Do you know who *Crazy Horse* is? ODB. That is why he had to play the *Heyoka* – the sacred clown dance in the

public domain where they have [him] classified as crazy. Who did he say was trying to kill him? He said Bush and his gang. What is he talking about? The *Deep State*; the *Illuminati*.

[Heyoka; (also spelled Heyokha, Haokah, and Heyokha) is a sacred clown in the culture of the Sioux (Lakota and Dakota people). Wikipedia]

269. **Herbert Walker Bush** was the leader of this part of the country - the world --for the Illuminati. He was the highest ranking member. How do I know this? Because if you read '*Behold the Pale Horse*', he gives the exact defense bill when he made himself King George of the United States and no other president could act without his permission. That means that everyone who came after him, until his death, was a puppet; Clinton, Bush Jr., and Bari whom you did not know that he had a Bush connection. *Barry Bel Soetoro*; Obama was his stage name in order to get the so called Negro vote and the uptown vote if he is approved by specific people he could get the party nomination.

[Born Barack Hussein Obama, II; Barry was a nickname and Soetoro was his stepfather's name.(Reuters)]; Bel?

270. Significance of number 19: Coming through numerology specifically Babylonian coming through Islam, 19 is the sacred seal—the alpha (1) and omega (9) is the Berth[ing] month. You seal it with the beginning and the end. If you add 1+9=10 the alpha going back to the beginning. It doesn't matter how you flip the number it represents what it says. The number 91, the blow up of the *World Trade Center in 911*. One of the Bin-Laden's died leaving the Bush resident in Texas. It is recorded. The Bin Laden's was the only plane that was allowed to leave America on 911. They had to be protected by the Bush family. Bin Laden was the masonic

connection in the Middle East because they got all the contracts to build the palaces in the Middle East in 1933 when they discovered there was oil in Saudi.

271. *The Nation of Islam started in 1933.* Most people do not look at the intricacies of the problem nor how to establish a solution. The only solution for us to stand up on our individual capacities and the Chief to come tell us where the imposters are at on the land, and get them out. That is what we need to know.

272. On Caucasians and balance: The Caucasians are not the problem. The problem is the ones who look like us but they are not us because they don't come from here. They are the problem. They know who they are and they can't stay. They tell all the time that they are leaving when you listen to their lies and they talk about leaving here. That is because they are part of the problem. That's why they can't stay. There were all skin colors of the people in the families of the Earth Tribes; all textures of hair. That is nothing new to us. What is new to us is to use those physical descriptions as tools of division. That is new to us.

273. Science on *Blue Star Kachina*: It's a Hopi prophecy of the red and blue stars of Kachina returning at the close of the Age for the rainbow children. They are just symbols to match the stellar of what is going on in time. They also made the Kachina doll of what takes place at that time. The say two stars will rise up; the red one, the blue one and those are the Kachinas.

274. *Shaman* verses *Heyoka*: A Shaman is an extreme empath who normally intersects more with the community than the Heyoka. When you see in the movies when they go

out into the woods to meet an old man [or woman] who lives by their self in the middle of nowhere. They could be a Heyoka or a Shaman. The medicine person of the village is the Shaman. When he or she gets struck on a prophecy, they go to the Heyoka to get assistance. In the Christian religion they would be called the *Melchizedek* Priests.

275. *Crypto Currency*: I do not advocate for any crypto currency because until this old system is done, I do not see which ones they have to undermine us and the ones they have developed to stay in the market. I don't trust none of them until we can see which ones they are.

276. Humans and water: Same connection as Mother to child. Water is a symbol of the spirit and is over 70% of the body and brain, and is natural anti-freeze in hot climate to stay cool, [and] in cold climate to stay warm. Water is critical to the survival of the body.

277. *Diamond child*: Clear with faint blue on the chakras; blue indigo energy.

278. Symbols: Important based on your learning style.

279. Conclusion: We didn't come on ships, we are not 'Black', we are not 'white', we are not crayons. We are organic to this land, we were already here before anyone named Christopher Columbus came snooping around to see how to take over our people. When we return back to our original oral tradition, we can chant down Babylon. The battle cry is "Free Larry Hoover." There are people who came over here and blended with our people. They are not our enemy but they are not our ally either because they want to carry on the narrative that the slave master gave us that we

come from Africa. So I just ask that they stay out of it and wait till we clean this mess up. We don't have hard feelings against them because they got invaded and colonized just like us. We just realize that we are not them and they are not us.

280. The family business now is to restore the Matriarchy, demand the three Kings, and protect the children. Anyone who can't vibe with that is not part of the family. These are the main glue points that bind us all together – Momma, babies, future. In our community, we don't talk back to our Mommas because we don't know how. That's just not our tradition. That not our culture. It's their [the colonizer's] culture. The way they rear their children is not the same as how we rear our children. We rear our children to withstand the most hostile of life conditions—of oppression, subjugation, infiltration, and subversions. We have to get out of it so that we can get our children out of it. The banana in the tail pipe is every divisive tool that they [invaders] can find. At one time all of the people of the world spoke the same language until someone named Yahweh divided up the languages. They say the devil main control is to divide and conquer. Who is he? In the *SumerianTablets* it says that Yahweh is Enlil, Lord [lowered; subordinate to the Creator] of the sky and booming voice; a jealous god. But we don't deal in jealousy because that is a toxic behavior that is contagious – passed on and taught. That is not natural to us. When you see us behaving out of jealousy, it is because we are trying to act like our oppressor. That is not part of our culture. I don't care if you have more or less than me, as long as you respect me like I respect you.

281. While we were worried about us respecting each other, they were worried about us having more than they got.

When they find out that they can't have what we got, now they are literally fighting for their life on Earth, or at least over here. I don't know where they are going, but they can't stay here. They have caused too many problems. They can feel it inside that they can't stay, and we can feel it in our soul that we are staying. We are not worried about your hurricanes, tornados, floods, [fires], because wherever they affect you is where the dirt is going down; and if some of us get caught up in the clean-up, Momma had to do it that way because she had to get the cancer out. That's how we look at it.

282. They look at it as "Oh no! We've got to stop the tornado with a bomb; you know they do have a tornado bomb. We don't pay attention because there are tornados in November, way pass tornado season, marching in mass in 'three strong' formation. That's Big Momma demanding the three Kings to bring balance back to Earth. Once Big Momma gets her seat and all of the Matriarchs get their posts across the land, the Chiefs job is to open the way. Not all Chiefs are men. There are more female than male Chiefs. *Chief War Horse* is a real Chief with the Blood that ties her to the land that knows our story. She comes from a long family of Chiefs. You can see her on *YouTube* explaining what happened to her people on the Trail of Tears and how they got separated from the $5 Indians that they used to switch us out. The problem is that in order for the $5 Indians to learn our culture, they had to put some of the elder women with them, priestesses, to teach them the traditions and the customs.

283. Now they know all of our customs and now they have to give it back. Big Momma said, when my babies come, then you have to give it back. They agreed. All of the treaties were made with $5 Indians, not with us. There is no record

of a treaty with Choctaw, Seminole, and Hopi. The only treaties were the largest of us that were able to be usurped. There were so many of us with so many different looks. That is why they called it the 'great melting pot' when they got here because we had all skin color and we lived peaceably. Then all of a sudden here comes these mfs and now there is no peace, we are oppressed, and we don't have Big Momma's [gold] money. This is where we are at. The unity in the community is the key to freedom. All of the indigenous land must [be] returned. Under the *[American] Indigenous Rights Act of 2016* they agreed to give it back. Also Washington D.C. has been closed for 2 years. All that we are seeing on T.V. now is a narrative that does not exist. All to distract us. The easiest way for us to get free is to say something at the same time in agreement.

CHAINS OF HELL; IT'S OVER

284. Governments of Earth are supposed to be Matriarchal because Earth is a feminine planet. So when they tried the Patriarchy, they created the deserts. Now my aim is to bring attention to the rise and return of the Matriarchy. People have this twisted idea of what the Matriarchy is. They think it's just [to] take all of the power from the men and replace it with powerful women. That is dumb to me. But what the Matriarchy really is about is [the] children because the Mothers know the children are the future and they teach this to the wise children that pay attention so when they grow up they [can] have a different world view. If our Mothers were teaching in the ways of woman, rather than what we see presently in this society [which] makes us greatly uncomfortable. If we don't study and develop a strong outlook from what we are seeing, we usually bug-out; we go

scary, riding around in the streets blasting one another because we don't know what else to do.

285. Don't fall for the fear campaign that the church, [and] the synagogue has been telling people for the last six thousand years of the chains of hell. Take the fear away and the chains become feathers. When we are looking at the personal development of individuals, they have to see someone who can see the problem and explain the problem for them [to be able] to see it. My job is to describe the problem and offer a solution where a solution is available. I haven't found a problem yet that was not solvable. One of the Elders said it better than anybody, "When all else fails, go back to nature because nature answers all of man's problems." We were answering problems before Silicon Valley, before Wall Street and Washington, and long before De Vatican. Mother Nature was answering the problems of everybody, [and] every place on the planet at all times.

286. So now our awareness will determine how fast this thing is moving. Apparently our awareness is reaching critical mass because they finally decided to tell all that their Queen is dead. A lot of people do not know that they gave a code sign when she passed when the crest on Buckingham Palace fell on the right side. That represents the right brain. The cress on the right side represents that the seal on the Mother side was broken. They were telling us that Elizabeth masquerading as the Queen was keeping the Queen disposed. We have to go into history to find something to compare it to. We compare it to the ousting of one Royal in order to replace them with another. We see a lot of it going on in Greece and Rome. A lot of people don't know we are still under Roman rule. Romans were called *Etruscans* before they established Rome. The *Etruscans* today are called

Moors. The Moors that were *Etruscans* came over as *Conquistadors*. We call them 'Dirty Moors' to distinguish them from what we call the 'Righteous Moors' who were the *Bey's* with the feathers who were fighting the *Conjure Wars* with the *El's* and the Fezzes.

287. The Righteous Moors job was to be properly educated in Moor history in order to know the difference between the organic people from the land over here, and those who came. We know for sure [that] we didn't have prisons before they came. When they came, they set up P.O.W. camps and called them plantations. In the after-mass, because as victors they got to write the history in a way to make us accept it as victors [also] even though we lost; but the war was [is] still going on. It went from a Bloody war, what we call the *Civil War* and the *GullahWars [to a Conjure War]*. The Gullah Wars – main street West Evers called it the *Seminole Wars*.

288. You can tell who is telling the story by what they call the war in the land of flowers [Florida]. If they call them Seminole Wars [they] are invaders. If they call them *Gullah Wars* or *Geechee Wars*, they are us telling what happened to us. Because we do not know the story correctly, because they intentionally with malice and forethought as they say in law, intentionally taught us wrong so that our perception of history and what happened to us would be clouded in a mystery. We were the masonic secret, and they wanted us to remain in perpetual ignorance as to who we were and our station on the land. *Big Momma* told me to get her –ish back and told me not to let anyone take my brother's and sister's – ish. When they told me that they stole my land, but I look out of my window and it is still here. I want to know where they put it. If the land is still here, even if they stole it, it is in the position for us to reclaim it.

289. This is what we have been working on. Everyone has got to do their part according to their level of overstanding. The higher your overstanding evolves, the more you are relied on to inform the collective clans across the lands of what we need to do as a people in order to face and overcome the threat. *Big Momma* always leaves us a way out no matter how big the problem we get into, no matter who comes here. She has one of her boys who are going to fix it. I'm number seven.

290. Columbus was a tawny Moor. He was mulatto. His boss was *Pedro Alonso Niño* D' Negro, a navigator on the ship. He was a Blackamoor. Because they have the same skin tones and hair texture as us, they can come and blend in with us and we won't know us from them. This was a challenge under George Washington.

[Pedro Alonso Niño; described as El' Negro was a Spanish navigator and explorer. He piloted the Santa Maria, accompanied by a crew of African descent, during Christopher Columbus's first voyage to the New World in 1492. Juan Niño, his brother piloted the ship La' Niña, which he also owned. A third brother, Francisco (youngest) was also on Columbus's voyage. The three were known as the Niño Brothers. (MelaninMindscape.com)]

291. In the **Six Fire Agreement known as the Paris Accord – we know it as the ***Treaty of Peace and Friendship*. The significance of that is the memorial that is left in Paris called the Eifel Tower and it's commemorating some one's fall [of] who's land it is on. Paris's full name is 'Parthenon Le' Isis' which means 'City of Isis.' So now you know that this was the fall of the Matriarchy that they are commemorating. But we have to have a tell coming from France to lay the book wide open. Do you know what the book would be? She carries it wide open in one hand and carries a light in the other hand

as a torch. [They call it Lady Liberty]. She has an old man face, but it has always been a man, because it represents the Pope. This is how you know – notice how she [stands] there with the book wide open. What book is it holding? Nobody knows what book is being held. It's the *Bible*. Why is she holding the Bible wide open? The *Bible* is no a spiritual text, it is a contract, a riddle, and a code for those who reach a certain attainment to follow a star map. In order to unlock the secrets of who we are.

**[The Treaty of Paris of 1783 formally ended the American Revolutionary War. The British recognized American Independence and ceded most of its territory east of the Mississippi River to the United States.(History.com)]

***[The Treaty of Peace and Friendship, also known as the Treaty of Marrakesh, was a bilateral agreement signed in 1786 between the United States and Morocco. (Wikipedia & Archives.gov)]

292. So the Pope, is masquerading in the Black Madonna seat as the Queen of Heaven and Earth. But he cannot sit on the real Queen seat. It is suspended thirty feet over his seat. If a man sits in the seat, they forfeit [the seat]. No man with testicles is supposed to sit in the seat, so they suspended it in the air so if the janitor mopping the floor doesn't get tired and say "I'm going to have a brief seat right here. In order to get up there you would have to have a thirty foot ladder.

293. What we use to call the 'House of Sybil' where the Oracle Priestess of the Earth fell up under what we call the Twelve Daughters of Isis, and they went to different regions of the world. Once they were trained to be a Matriarch they helped everybody else with their spiritual development. All of this got hi-jacked by Yahweh – Zeus – Enlil – Alexander's father. This is who Hebrew Israelites, Muslims, Jehovah's Witness, (Jehovah is a rendition of Yahweh) worship. Those who know this is not telling it.

294. In the news, the so-called Indians met with the Pope in Canada [July 24-29, 2022]. There was a lady who put the Pope on notice in the public domain. Because we couldn't get close enough to put him on notice, we had to send the ones that they made contracts with. They did not make contracts with us. We didn't sign treaties and contracts because those contracts they were offering went against the moral code of the land. So they created $5 Indians so that they could have someone to sign these treaties that we refused to sign. That is why they set up the reservations for them and left us in Arkansas, Alabama, Mississippi, and Louisiana instead of funneling us back to our lands. They say that the Pueblo Natives just disappeared – like poof—off the Earth. No! When we go to war, the whole family goes. We drop the babies off at Big Momma's house. Big Momma has the aunties there to take care of the babies while we go fight the war, and we leave men at Big Momma's house. Well, they hijacked Big Momma's house, took her name out and called it the 'Big House', and labeled our family plats as plantations. Now we don't even want to go back home. The Blackamoors helped them to do this.

295. When you look at the Washington [Masonic] Memorial in D.C., you have a whole lot of fezzes in there. They are the ones who challenged us to the Conjure Wars. They are the El's and they all are under a 'Death Oath'. That is why there is a sword on every one of those fezzes to not tell us who we are and to replace us. They are not us. They want to replace us. They have never been us. They just look like us. The Natives of this land are more tied to the people of Polynesia and East Asians than they are to Africans. That does not mean that we don't have African Blood because on the Atlantic we had been doing trade with Africa for thousands of

years on the east coast from north to south. Then we were doing trade with China, Japan, and other islands for thousands of years. They have ancient ships from China that date back to a couple thousands of years. They also have ships from Africa like *Mansa Musa* who sailed over here. They also got [the ship of] the Pharaoh who also sailed over here for vacation, but we don't got any slave ships. None of the slave ships they told us about exists. We cannot find any of them; none from Africa and none from over here. They tell us that the Africans sold their own people, but the ones here don't look like the ones that they are bringing.

[(Below) Tippu Tip; also known as Muhammed bin Hamid, born 1837, of Zanzibar, was the most famous 19th century Arab trader. (Cambridge.org & Britannica)]

296. Look at *Tippu Tip*. *Tippu Tip* doesn't identify as being an African. He self identifies as being an Arab. The term Arab means wanderer. Elijah Muhammad said "Everywhere they go they cause mischief and Bloodshed." They have no place [that] they are native to because they are not native to anywhere on the planet. So they go amongst peaceful people and start conflicts and then offer a solution to the conflict that they started, for a fee. They look like us, but they are not us. Their hearts don't feel like our hearts feel. We operate from a place of love, compassion, and generosity. They operate from a place of hate, misery, and deception. They came here dark skinned. They are from *Nibiru*. Nibiru has all skin tones of people. The respect that they have for each other is similar to the respect that we have for one another. But the respect that they have for us is zero. We are pets to them, those of us who are melanated and non-melanated. They see us as pets and farm animals to be farmed for food. Adrenochrome is not the only secretion that they extract. All of your glands have different secretions

under certain conditions. They will activate a certain gland so that the secretion is the heaviest in the Blood. That is why it's good to know what your glandular systems. They want you pituitary, thyroid, pancreas; they want them all.*[Nibiru; (Neberu, Nebiru)is of the Akkadian language, meaning 'crossing' or 'transition point.' A visible astronomical object that marks an equinox. Babylonian culture identifies Nibiru as "Marduk's Star."(Wikipedia)]*

297. When you were growing up in church and talked about the war in heaven, and Satan was cast to hell and bound for four thousand years; that was Enlil's son Marduk that was bound in the Antarctic. He is no longer there. His job when he came here was to do all that he could to enforce the laws of the Galactic Council, by his father's orders. His father was trying to take over Earth. Marduk did not want to be here. He was a high ranking military official on Nibiru with great skills on military strategy, deception, and he was proficient at making people lose their minds based on living conditions. This is what they have been doing. Marduk, being chained in the Antarctic, Tehuti sent his brother [also named] Marduk, Enki's son to Nibiru to secure Nibiru. [He then] changed the name of Nibiru to Marduk to let us know on Earth that the Marduk we sent to Nibiru [has] secured, so that Enlil could not take two places over at once. He would take over [only] one of them or nothing, but not both. The Marduk we sent to Nibiru came back as *Malachi York*.

298. Marduk who was Enlil's son had people he could telepathically control as if he were them. All this is in hieroglyphs and cuneiform and that is why they did not want us to learn [these languages].

299. Arab means 'wonderer', but you've got different tribes. Chaldean means 'people of the plains.' They are closely

related to the Arab, but are a different tribal group and their religion is Christianity, Catholic; whereas the Arab religion is Islam and they follow *Ninersin who replaced *'Allat'* as the god of the Arabs from Matriarchal to Patriarchal. *Allat* was the moon goddess, but now Allah is the moon god. I still say Goddess.

300. *Sister Pruitt*: I tell people that Allah is *******Allat*, but they do not listen to me.
Rod: They do not do any research. They just go by what people tell them [and accept it] as the gospel truth. They are as much educated about Islam as the average Christian over here is about Christianity. If they do not lace the lie with some truth [people] are not going to fall for it at all.
*[Ninisina; (Sumerian) Mesopotamia goddess; daughter of Anu; deity of the city Isin, considered a healing deity.
**[Allat; also spelled al-Lat, Ellat; is an ancient Goddess of pre-Islamic times, associated with the god Dhu-shara, known as Allah (supreme god). (encyclopedia.com)]

301. *Rod*: When *Larry Hoover* first got locked up in 1973, he denounced the 'gangster disciples' then and we know if the masters are observing, you have to come out of the situation and say the same thing you said going in. That is how you know that it is up, so the statement that he put out denouncing gangster disciples is nothing new to us, but growth and development which is a graduated ideology from gangster disciple community terrorist trained by the government to terrorize our own people, to wait a minute, something is going on. We are not gang banging anymore, we are 'brain banging' now.

302. He has said to the government agents that he is not a gangster disciple; that he advocates 'growth and development' which is predicated on the principles of self-

knowledge and self-development by erudition and self-learning. We do not advocate anyone terrorizing our community because the first chance [that] we get we need to snuff that –ish out. They were never organized in the beginning to be community terrorists. They were originally organized to protect the community against the tyranny of the mfs with the badge who were terrorizing the community, [and] that caused the cohesion amongst the youth. The government turned them into gangs through infiltration. We have verification of that during the so-called Rodney King riots when they called the peace treaty between the Bloods and the Crypts. Then the police came through dressed like Bloods shooting up the Crypts and the Bloods that they said [did it] was in the party. So they tell the Crypts to fall back; they are false flagging [us]. We are figuring to find out what it is. There were four people in the car, and two of them were FBI agents. Two of them were from the Rampart Crash Division of Gang Task Force. They need us to fight each other.

303. Laws in Chicago: They are trying to make them straight. What they would do in Chicago was to make them change the laws on the bonds. They have a 21 year old dude that the police can't get off the streets, and they catch him with a pistol. The pistol has a 25 year old murder on it. He's in possession of the pistol. They charge him with the murder, when they know there is no way possible that he could have committed the murder because he wasn't born yet. But they will hold him without a bond and give him court continuances for as long as they could. According to his knowledge of the law, his lawyer his lawyer is part of it [the set up]. But now we say "no", because the constitution guarantees you a reasonable bond. They never honor that, so now they give

everybody a personal bond. It's not as clean cut as people are making it. So, they might say that [someone] committed a second degree murder and got a personal bond, so I'll be out in the morning. That may happen once, but try it again; it won't happen again. These laws are designed to be to our detriment. Any law they pass is not to our benefit. They never passed a law with the organic people of the land in mind, except to subjugate us.

304. When the Supreme Court ruled way back in the early days that we would never be part of this country; that we would always be a perpetual enemy combatants; that is an old Supreme Court ruling that has never been rescinded, and they have a doctrine in law called *'*Stare Decisis*'* which means' direct look' if it hasn't been over turned, it is still in effect. Dred Scott is still in effect. If you are $3/5^{th}$ compromised, you are an 'imbecile in law' and have no Rites [nor rights] that a free white person is obligated to respect... The only thing is that you don't even know that a free white person is a Moor. It's right in the *Black's Law Dictionary* as a category of Moor – free white person. So when we [are] thinking that they are talking about pale skin people, the white man isn't even white. [It is] that Nigger [who is] blacker than me and you; it's a term that indicates nobility.*[Stare Decisis'; is a legal doctrine that obligates courts to follow historical cases when making a ruling on a similar case. (Investopedia.com)]*

305. We fought back. We have never stopped fighting. We never signed a treaty. We just had to change our strategy of the fight because it was decimating both sides to [the point of] annihilation. We know that at the close of the Age, we can get them [the inorganic] off the planet, but we have to survive long enough to do that. So that is what made us

accept the *Conjure War* which put us all in amnesia. We [are] gods with amnesia, walking around with dementia and don't even know it.

306. Russia: They are not about to come over here. All that saying "China is about to invade", "Russia is about to invade", is straight out of the 48 Laws of Power – the boogey man. We have to create a boogey man for you all to be scared of so that you all can run to these cowards for protection. Stop falling for the fear campaign.

**[THE PLAN] aka; WHERE IS ALL THE BEEF?
w/ Rod & Taj Tarik Bey**

307. Taj: From the beginning, and although I would tell people in different forums at different times, not only did they breach the contract in the later years, they breached from the beginning, however, the people kept calling them their government, "my senator", etc. They have no relationship to us in that sense, only obligations. And even though there are *de facto *Shakums* who made treaties with them, the implied existence of, and obligation was pressed upon us, when we actually had no party in it. And you know, and I knew that culturally we could never sell the land – that is number one; so any transfers that they are proclaiming was fraudulent. The problem that we had was that our people kept giving it validity. And so I would present issues to them that would always prove that as soon as you present an issue of truth, you would start getting counter measures coming from them and coming from people on our side who pretended to be caring about our people. But in doing so, they would be exposing themselves. I already knew the contract was dead. The contract was dead before it began. However, it only lives because the heirs kept believing in them. The same way the heirs keep believing in the priesthood, not knowing that the priesthood is part of the problem, and the people don't know that but the politicians, the clergy, the Imams, and the *Rabbis*, and many of the *Sheiks* and *Shakums* are part of a network that operate together against the interests of the aboriginal people. And so, this is why, over the years, to counter the Barbary instruments that harbor Europeans and United State companies operating from Switzerland and also from Austria, etc. that they were using on the stock market. If I can get the people to stop putting instrumentalities into the public domain that would counter them, or that would be claiming the estate, it would be messing with the stock market and all of the instrumentalities that they created under the Fourteenth Amendment fiction of war ship status that they have our people in. And at the same time they would counter or reject or try to dismiss, it would show the people their belligerent FOFA operations. And so we always promoted for the people to go into the ancient and a modern jurisprudence in order to recognize both the terms and legalities and making the distinctions between legal operations and the lawful operations. So that the people can start thinking critically, which you already know that our people have long since stopped thinking critically. They think on emotions and belief systems which they don't know is MK-Ultra and animal husbandry training set up by John D. Rockefeller and Frederick T. Gates.*[De facto; in reality; not formally recognized; resulting from social factors, not from laws or actions of the state. (Merriam Webster)]*

308. This is why I always told them a lot of things that we are doing we will not be doing later because I already knew that when the time comes, when the people got conscious, that not only was the contract dead, they were never obligated to

it. The only obligation part is of article 3, section 2, and article 6 where the treaties, and anything that was valid that was their obligations superior to their operations here, and as soon as the people see they never honored that, what more do the people need to recognize that these people are absolutely de facto. However, with the recognition that all the Shakums around the land (of whom we call Chiefs) job was to step up and speak up. I was kind of disappointed relative to a lot of these Grand Chiefs and different brothers and sisters that were coming up along the way that knew the fundamental principles, of whom I will not name. But I understood when Malcom started to recognize some of this stuff that had much to do with why they murdered him because he would not sell out. [Rod: Malcolm was not murdered by pale skin Europeans].

309. I was disappointed recognizing persons who were put in place who was supposed to step up and do exactly what you said and what you are doing, in –not the Moors Science Temple of America, that's a corporate side – the Moors Holy Temple of Science, they were charged to step up, and they didn't. We don't have to get into the Eisenhower administration – you know, the multi-level stuff that took place there. Even within that venue, when they relinquished jurisdiction at *Al Maghrib*, so now the corporate *Morocco* was politically relinquished and therefore *Al Maghrib*, or the organic people of the land, have the right and obligation to step up.

310. Principle: When you [Rod] stepped up and made what is called a reversion of a state, because this is the rule, and you know it and I know it, but for the people who are listening, cause when you are dealing with TRUST or you are

dealing with inheritance you are dealing with generational issue of obligation. The obligation of an interregnum government or an occupational government, which is temporary, is to preserve or protect the estate, until such said competent heir speaks up. It must be public, it can't be secret, and it must be transparent. However, the assumptions that a lot of people have that you have got to have some title or that somebody has got to tell you this or that – no! It has got to come divinely. And the greatest divine gate that we have here in the physical form at mid-guard is your Mother! When you [Rod] started talking Matriarchy in principle of law, because anyone of us with the *Rite of Blood* could have done it. They failed to do it. Because you did it that came from [the] divine. When it was presented to you, and you accepted your obligation, etc., it is valid. The other issue is that through the Shakums around the land, whose obligation is to that support, and that is what we are to do at this point on. It is said, so let it be. I relieve the floor.

311. *Rod*: One of the things in our thinking called the 'paralysis of analysis.' It is not enough to have the Blood and the Rite, you have got to have the knowledge of the application of the Blood Rite. Having a good overstanding of civics is the first order of business that was given to us by the prophet Noble Drew Ali when he said "Get you a good Moorish education, get you a good civics education." In the process of learning these things, he said that he was going to leave these people in power long enough to learn how to run a government. And he said the number of people that were going to make it would be only a handful. He said to be careful because your own brother will sell you into slavery. We had to be cautious, we had to talk to each other without being able to be in the same room at the same time. So we

talked through the signs and through the symbols. Some people take the dogma to be the doctrine, but the doctrine is concealed in the dogma. Morals and Dogma by Albert Pike is the manner by which they rule us. Jacobites, Yakub [who is] Jacob undermined our morals by replacing them with dogma. Noble Drew Ali said beware of religious controversy. Religious controversy is predicated upon arguing dogma. All religions are dogmatic because they are social control mechanisms that have nothing to do with the spiritual development of people.

312. *Taj*: Yes, they are called the 'three S's'; Social Solis Systems.
Rod: So I gained sufficient knowledge, enough to meet the challenge knowing the date that the contract is going to close. How do I know the date? Because I have the Blood and the Rite to establish the date. When I established the date, I had a knock back receipt from the Republican Party honoring that, when on July 4, they did an inaugural debate with no flag, and a blue backdrop.
Taj: Yeah, and how many people paid attention to that?
Rod: That's my job. And the blue background, I'm from the blue house, a growth and development baby, a brain banging offspring from Larry Hoover's family tree. I have been tested and put through the fire by people linked to Angel Bey's soldiers on the street. They are still there to tell the story. Because in order to establish the Blood Rite, all of the Chiefs had to send somebody to examine me. And then they had to pass and prove me. So, when the bikers made the truce with Angel Bey and Larry Hoover, none of the regular people know it, but I had to be approved by Bikers to be the redeemer of the family tree. I can't redeem the blue side without redeeming the red side because that's my Momma's side.

My father's side is the blue side. So when the blue got flipped to the red, I became my Momma's right hand man. When they ask me where I come from, I proceeded to come forth from the right hand of God. Ain't no dispute about it, pick up your book and read where I am supposed to come from. Big Momma gave me instructions to leave no stone unturned. Each stone represents one of the Priestesses (or Princesses) on the land. I've got to find them. I've got to know who the Grand Matriarch on the land is. Because I have got to tell everybody who she is; that is Farrakhan's wife. She has the Blood and the Rite; she has the most matriarchs under her direction.

313. *Taj*: You know the rule – it has nothing to do with ego, which you already know. It has to do with the natural response of respect from the women around her in numbers and they will demonstrate it in general. It has to be a natural response, it can't be artificial.

Rod: Those women we call *MGTGCC*. That is how the Matriarchs establish how to tie back into the vine, or the main family line. So, the *MGT* (Muslim Girls Training), they are the ones that offered the *GCC* (General Civilization Class). *Elijah Muhammad* was teaching these women how to raise a nation, not how to raise a baby. That is the difference, nation.

Taj: This is for the people; nation, nativity, nationality, means to be born to come into life; that's the relationship. When we talk nationality, we are not talking paperwork; we are talking honor of your Mother, honor of your inheritance, claim of your inheritance, Rite of your inheritance, Rite of heritability and competence to claim your inheritance and your connection to law; that is land, air, and water at midguard. So therefore, a competent heir must speak up to the belligerent faux-fers for the estate to be released. Other point which you [Rod] have already made and which we already knew long ago, is this goes beyond the fiction of George Washington, the ninth pradorey, of their corporation, converting our honorvilles into their corporate states, stealing our estates, selling out, etc. as you already know [that] he had a little bit of Moorish Blood in him anyway.

314. Rod: They replaced the real George Washington with Albert Pike.

Taj: Basically they are about the same people. They just removed the beard. But the deal of it is, and this is mainly for the people, because they really need to comprehend where you are coming from. They think there is a conflict. There is not a conflict, there is a level of overstanding what has been said to you over the years from the beginning. People don't know what Estate is, they don't know what TRUST is, they don't know what governmental obligations are, they don't know what constitutions are, they don't know about *Ghidhnaea,* the great tree where we always meet, they don't know about the great principles that honor human rights, etc. that are peppered within that constitution came from us, that's not their stuff. They just use that instrument to claim authority which they never honored, because it did not come from them in the nature of everything. However, there's two keys in there that locked them in. That is why they never respected it. And it never gave us Rites, it puts obligations on them as faux-fers to preserve Rites that already belong to us. This is why when they had the ordinance of 1777, to formulate the Republican form of government, they could not even operate unless they maintained a Republican form. And with that Republican form, they must honor the treaties that are superior. And so even the treaties that were falsely presented put obligations on them, which is why they have never respected them. This is also why they never teach civics or real history, or [about] the wars, or [of] the trading's, or of the ancient Canaanites, Moabites, etc., and [of] our travels across the waters for centuries – not a couple hundred years, for millennia. They took over our trade routes and claimed them to be theirs and it's really our stuff; not only the material, even the trade route. But someone had to speak up. Noble Drew Ali spoke up in proper person. Now here you [Rod] come speaking up in proper person. You must be heir, you must have the Blood, you must have the Rite of claim, and you must make that claim. You cannot be non-transparent.

Rod: At that point that makes me contender to the throne.

Taj: Exactly.

315. *Rod*: And as contender to the throne, now we have to explain the difference in nationality under 'Amorite Law' verses the 'Law of the Land.' You [already] gave them the 'Law of the Land.' The Amorite jurisdiction that we were artificially under, this is where the problem, and the disconnect come in. Under them when you are trying to become a National under Amorite Law, you fall under the jurisdiction of Uniform Commercial Code. Becoming a National under the Amorite gives them the proof that they need that you are imbecile in law and therefore cannot manage your own estate [or affairs]. So we have to come from superior jurisdiction in order to over throw this inferior [government].

316. *Taj*: This is why people must know the distinction of what Noble Drew Ali did when he set up the Moors Holy Temple of Science Civic Organization, distinguished from The Moors Scientific Temple of America that is the corporate arm (i.e.) under the Amorite jurisdiction to make a counter measure to Roosevelt using all of the peoples birth

certificates and marriage certificates, etc. to back their private debt. After they went bankrupt again in [19]25 and covered up in [19]28, and then he adopted that religious affidavit as a political move; that is not a divine move, which is a political move by necessity. Then people tried to make that dogmatic position of arguing a religious argument for the Moorish movement. The Moorish movement is separate from the Moors Science Temple of America. The movement is for humanity. The movement is for the organic man [to be] distinguished from the corporate venue or the CORPORATE [straw] man. I think a lot of people really still don't get it, but I'm glad and I'm grateful that you [Rod] have the mind and the critical will to speak up and make that clear to the people, because that is absolutely true. If you are talking about the organic people, you are talking about the *Al Maghrib*; if you are going to talk about the corporate venue that's Morocco, etc. That venue is dead. That is only for the seas or under what they call the Holy Sea; we are not just talking about the water, or Amorite Law, we are talking about the Pope of Rome. Someone had to speak up and dethrone their claim of *Unum Sanctum, Dom Devers's, Enter Catered Venom, Univac, Al De 'Bulls*, and all the bullshit that went with it.

317. *Rod*: And I did that and it's also recorded in the public domain. I went after the three city-states, and when I overthrew De Vatican this is when they started using the holographic Pope. When I overthrew the Queens palace over in Europe that is when the cress fell off of the gate [and] it's still ain't up there.

Taj: And they talk about they're still remodeling.

318. *Rod*: And when I put the claim in to reclaim the government that was your June 6 episode when we had to put a red flag behind the Amorite flag at *Pelosi's* desk which was the seat of political power for the corporation in order to claim the seizure of her ship that they claim we crashed into. We see then somebody that look like them but he was trained by us. He had to put it in the public domain that he was working for us and he did that. Then he had to go in there with the flag with no fringe, stake the claim by staking the flag behind the desk and occupy the territory. It could be [as little as] five minutes, and we win. So what did they do? They left with the podium. These are all political power moves being played out base on claiming the land and restoring the balance to nature according to the laws of nature in the orders of the *Grand Matriarchs* across the land. They all agree that they are tired of the B.S., of going to baby's funerals, they are tired of burying their daughters and their daughters coming up missing, misused, neglected and abused. They told me to do something about it. At the time [that] they told me, I didn't know what they were talking about because I was three. I didn't know what they were talking about, but I figured it out.

Taj: Under the guise of global warming, they slaughtered over 20 thousand heads of beef.

319. *Rod*: All of those GMOs, I told them they had to go. I said that over a year ago, all GMOs had to go, all the bovine growth hormone infected beef had to go. They are not feeding that to the people anymore, not under my watch. So now if you look around over the last two years you will find out all these food places they have been destroying are GMO and hormone productions that are not going to be allowed.

Taj: If anyone is paying attention, all of those arch signs on all of those burger joints, they are taking them all down. So a lot of the patterns for all the venues around the world are being demonstrated from Russia.

320. *Rod*: A lot of people don't know that Wall Street is being seized. All that is playing out of Wall Street now is being used to steer public opinion. Wall Street was seized for laundering and concealing trillions of dollars from trafficking money. So, I already told them to seize Wall Street, but also, they have something called the International Stock Exchange. They trade globally. They were also audited and found to be laundering drug money and illegal gun running, and trafficking, so we seized that –ish too. When they were telling us that Russia was invading Ukraine, they were closing down laboratories that were making poison to kill us over here. So all the time they are not tell you, [and] you are not watching the signs and symbols, because when the Barbados thing came up, when they told us that the Queen no longer had jurisdiction in Barbados, the Barbados flag waves the flag colors of Ukraine which tells Russia when to make the move. Barbados had the trident and Ukraine has the eagle in form of the trident as their symbols. The flags go in two different directions; that means two different moves have to take place, one behind the other. So now we are following the science of flag study – the law of the flag.

321. Our people over here are totem pole and feather people. But the rest of the world is flag people. Even though we are totem pole people, the responsibility of the Chief is to know how to read the flag. That's how you track the pirates to the skull and bones society and George H. W. Bush to the

Senate Select Committee that gave him jurisdiction as King George the first of the United States of America as written by William Cooper (to be verified and sent in document) in *Behold the Pale Horse*. When he did that, the next following three presidents, he had picked them; his son (G. W. Bush), his adopted son Wm. Jefferson Clinton and his adopted daughter Hillary Rodham Clinton known for the drug running and trafficking in Arkansas before he was ever considered for president with the CIA going on a massive cover-up campaign leaving a trail of bodies to conceal the drug trafficking while they got Angel Bey and Larry Hoover sitting in prison so they can't exercise the Rites over the land as a bond servant. So that is why when I gave them the orders to release the political prisoners, I had to call Angel Bey by name, and I had to call Larry Hoover by name, and I had to identify that Stan T. Williams was not executed but that he was put in cryostasis. So then I had to give them an order to thaw him out.

322. If they don't know the signs to read, then they don't know how to make all of these necessary claims to re-establish the de- jure' over the de facto. When we are overthrowing the corporate jurisdiction of Amorite Law. I'm following all the steps. They just don't know what needs to be done. My Elders told me "Rod, if you know the way, then you have to lead." If they haven't done it yet, it is only because they don't know. None of us like this bull-ish. Me being 100% dissatisfied, we are not leaving this world like this for my children to have to deal with the same isms that we have been dealing with. So then I have to exercise my jurisdiction from divine law and divine Birth Rite.

323. In the ancient code of Kings is where it is codified. But the ancient code of Kings is concealed by the royal families. So now I have to remember the ancient code of Kings from past incarnations so that I can exercise the first Rite of jurisdiction of the Birth Rite of the Earth which goes to my sisters. So I have to fight for my sister's stuff and when my sisters get theirs they will take care of me till mine comes. All of the work that I am doing, the only people that don't overstand what needs to be done is the ones complaining. I did the work and I exercised the jurisdictional claims of Birth Rite, I overthrew De Vatican, then through the military industrial complex, I had to go one on one with artificial intelligence, they said if I could not beat A.I. we were going to move to a technocracy. They gave him four points of quantum encryption. I came in at 12 points of quantum encryption. The A.I. couldn't keep up. It started spitting out gibberish to them because it can't translate what I am saying when I give a knock to a knock back on a monkey flip—on a master grip, the computer already lost. They can't keep up with the god mind of a god man. Finally it realized god form and god mind. So now they can go take their A.I. and put that on the side and use it to educate our children like joisting, so they can get their god mind opened by going against the computer. That's all it is, it's the mind against the computer; the machine; the matrix. The matrix is inside of the mitochondria. If you don't overstand the mitochondrial Birth Rite to the Earth, then you are stuck in the matrix and can't get out, and by unlocking the matrix you unlock the mitochondria, you unlock the Blood of the sisters.

Taj: Yep. They have been giving the whole world a false Mother, because the Mother is the inheritance.

324. *Rod*: Right, and they've been giving them a Dragon B.; and Archon with reverse genetic material. We've got xx & xy; she's got xx & yx. Her boys look like girls and their girls look like boys.

Taj: That is why they have been practicing that cross-gender practice in order to kill the Matriarchy and create a false reality of their artificial A.I. womb.

325. *Rod*: But you can never replace Momma. One thing we need is to not send anyone else to the hospital to have a baby without a sister or Momma in the room with her. Stop letting them cut the umbilical cord before the baby suckles. The colostrums and the oxytocin goes through the system of the baby and tells the mother that the baby was successfully delivered. When they cut the cord before that process takes place, the placenta tells the mother that she had a miscarriage, but her physical eyes are looking at the baby creating an internal conflict into post-partum depression. We have got to get out of that practice as soon as possible. We have got to get out of their educational systems because those are training facilities for their plantations – animal husbandry. Skinner box and response education; training you how to be in their system. Those who don't want to comply, they throw them in the penitentiary.

326. The Three Kings job is to report what is going on with the water, the land, and the air, and with the people. From there they clear the way for the Matriarchal to be seen in the public in order to re-establish the jurisdiction – de jure. They are working hand in hand.*[De jure; Latin for 'by law']*

Taj: When Brother Rod is saying Larry Hoover, you've got to look at the meta-physicality of what he is saying. He's not just talking about Larry himself; he's talking about the principle of the non-jurisdictional incarceration of both Larry, the non-jurisdictional suppression of the *Moabitess* or the *Circle of Mothers*, the non-jurisdictional action on political prisoners in general, and the restoration of their obligation as belligerent faux-fers, to release the estate and to stop perpetrating the fraud on humanity as a nation or government, all of which they are not and never have been. According to the rule of international law it is actually their obligation to assist what is going on right now, and they are even breaching that. However, I am glad that Brother Rod has stepped up as he has, because basically what he is doing is what the Grand Chiefs were assigned to do by Noble Drew Ali in act one of the Moors Holy Temple of Science. They were the ones who were to step up but of course we already know the history on that.

327. *Rod*: One thing that Noble Drew Ali said, was that he was going to leave them in power long enough for us to learn how to run a government. Any of the Grand Chiefs that didn't do the work means that it wasn't their job at that time. Because they couldn't be competent to this level and refuse to do the work because it's the only way to give the collective the relief. Respecting the fact that, and I tell people all the time that I'm not a Moor, but I'm a student of Moors Science, and my overstanding of Noble Drew Ali's intent is for them people to stay in power long enough for us to learn how to run a government. We can run it now. We don't need nobody's help. We don't need no de facto corporation that

was set up as an interim government. We don't need them anymore. They can go now.

Taj: We need more alpha males to step up to protect the Mothers to make them feel more comfortable to take their position and not be distracted by the B.S. coming from the culture that is here.

328. *Rod*: When you were saying the meta-physics that was involved in the Free Larry Hoover, I keep telling everybody it's not only Larry Hoover. Free *Larry Hoover* is the one condensation that everyone can get on the same page with, along with free *Malik Angel Bey*, free *Mumia Abu-Jamal*, bring *Assata Shakur* back home, release all the of our political prisoners...and to raise and restore the Matriarchs. We've made agreements across all of our Chiefs; the Chiefs overstand, but now we are on the *Juneteenth* campaign to inform the grass roots that the corporate system is over. What you are looking at on T.V. is a stage play played out as a tool of distraction so that you don't know that it's time for you to walk off the job, having been hired for a month or two and come all the way out. But nobody is gonna want to do that, but it's gonna get harder before it gets easier. If you look at the senates and congresses across the country, they've got senators and congress men walking off the job all because it's over. Everybody on the land has to be accounted for with the Chiefs. There's no clans on the land, whether they are Bikers, KKK, Moor Science Temple, whether they are Growth and Development, they all have to have somebody as a representative or in the collective of the clans. You can't clean this-ish up taking sides. That is why it's a round table, not a square table. The one whose job it is, is the one who knows how to perform that function. They are going to be ascribed titles according to their function. Even the red lodge

call Larry Hoover *Chief Hoover* or the *Chairman*. That means when it comes time to restore the land, that's the Chief that Big Momma appointed to speak up for the collective. [You] cannot take sides with nobody's B.S., get in the middle of the drama and say "it's not going down like that." This is what's really going on, on the land. I'm reading it like I'm reading a book, because I know our culture well enough to know that it's in transitional phase. The FEMA document maps out the strategy for the transition of the government. Don't argue with me, argue with the document. The document gave us a clear cut description. We've seen the movement. Larry Hoover's lawyer went to see him last month, but he couldn't see him because he wasn't there. They in continuity of government, waiting on the people to get on the same page so that we can start following the carrot on the stick, and we can get to the goal line.

Taj: They can't give reparations: #1 it ain't theirs to give, #2 our people are the people of the land, and have been refugees in our own land. We need to recognize that and step up.

329. *Rod*: Restoring the land is more important than me fighting with the Dirty Moors and me telling them that I listen to Taj. We know from history that there are some people on the land that look like us, that murder us when we reach positions of prominence. The look just like us, but they ain't us. They've shown their hand. These are people who came over calling themselves Conquistadores. They tutor royal family members, hide out in Switzerland, live in upstate New York and New Jersey in gated communities. All that has been busted up, but everybody's watching the dog and pony show, the holographic images and the actors playing Joe Biden. This –ish is over with.

330. Dr. G & Taj: In review of the [online] comments, there is so much negativity and I think it's because you speak with so much confidence and assurety on what folks are finding incredulous, and therefore they think that you [Rod] are crazy for you to say "I did this, I did that, I shut down Buckingham Palace." Yet we should be happy that someone (in the person of Rod Hayes) took the initiative to do it [what needed to be done]. I'm reminded of what *Grand Chief Doryah Bey* did in 2013, there was a number of paper work that expired and she had to do certain things that no one had done at that point.

Taj: That was the Moors Science Temple of America where they had let the corporate papers expire.

Dr. G: Yes, no one stepped up to the plate, because it was a one hundred year charter. She did it, and she still gets to this day flak over her calling herself who she is as Prime Minister.

Taj: People did not overstand a government action. Even though, from the corporate perspective all that stuff is dead now and not necessary. The principle of her recognition was to try to set a platform correct so that she could start cleaning up the misrepresentation. However, the reality of it is that as the people become more and more conscious the people need to recognize that the corporate platform and all bondry [boundary] instruments related to it, which Brother Rod is making reference to, are dead and unnecessary. What is necessary is for the people to now come back to their tribal clans and go back to the principles like Noble Drew Ali said, "go back to the state of mind of your ancient Mothers and Fathers," because our concepts are all wrong. He said at the same time some things have to be presented to the people in the nature of what they were used to, but he also said that the half has not yet been told. So you can start practicing or exercising your critical mind and you will find there are other things that you needed. That is why you never stand still. That is why you never take a position; you don't take sides and you stick with principles and in time the principles will show you everything you need to know. Organizations are not set up to live forever. They are set up to do a job, but the job is what you call an abstract, just like customs and traditions are what you call abstract miscellaneous (trinkets, statues, different things that were made by our forefathers is what you call corporal objects), but abstracts can be done in the building of the character of the mind. You must recognize that when that is recognized, those physicality's are unnecessary. People think that the organization is the thing, but the organization is a tool. When the job is done, the tool is put away. People have looked at the Moors Science Temple as the nation; it is not. It is an outreach venue put in place for communication and to deal with the corporate side of our activities that were forced into, not to be continued [indefinitely]; it passes on. The job is done, which is why we are even having this conversation. You don't maintain the job [when it is complete], you maintain the principle. Maxims are principles that are based in nature laws that don't pass away. That's why you take your position based on principles in order to vet all that you do – left or right. You don't take a position, you don't take sides, you take principle and you stand on that principle because we, basically in our physical form are fickle, and we change up because of this. We put faith in people based on what organization they belong to when we start giving importance to organizations more than they deserve. What Noble Drew Ali did one hundred years ago has served its purpose, and is why Rod did what he did, whether it came from him or anyone else, that principle of that claim still stands, it needed someone to recognize it. People look at images, thinking someone is supposed to come in silk suits, with diamonds around their wrists. Guess what, Brother Rod comes and he is so down to Earth that it makes some people feel uncomfortable. He is so real about it, and blunt about it, and alpha about it, that it makes some people who don't have testicles uncomfortable. Rather than them admit that they haven't done their job, they want to attack the messenger. He's not worried about it and neither am I. Get the work done, and we don't need a damned title [to get it done]. Thank you so much. [People] are mixing pedigree with corporate activity. They do not overstand that the Moors Science Temple is a corporate action done by political necessity. It does not supersede nor does it give pedigree. Moor is Moroccan for *Al Moroccan*, Al [Mooreaux or Mooru (sp.?)], referring to all of the *Bantu, Mandingo, Phoenicia, Aegypta,* etc. which are Africans around the world; it is a general cover of African clans. It is not directly a nationality in a sense that people think that it is. It is a jurisdictional designation. When Noble Drew Ali set up the jurisdiction of Moorish American, that is to distinguish the Birth Rite clans of the aboriginal people distinguished from other Moors around the world, some of who has been trying to make claims here that do not have a claim. [Moorish American] is a political distinction. It does not make you who you are, you are already who you are. It was just a political necessity. Canadian is a corporate entity too [same as the U.S. corp.] that has also been defunct. *Canada Corporation* and *United States Corporation* have the same international number. They both are property of the Queen. They are not really the organic land. People need to make the distinction between the organic land, the organic people, and the corporate land names. People think that we are rejecting their nationality when nationalities only indicate political jurisdictional venues. The organic is distinguished from the corps, or the dead. That is why Noble Drew Ali gave to us the allegory of 'black' according to science means death. [Here] he is talking from a social engineering principle. This is why he said "every temple must have a school." These things were not done. The world doesn't stop because things that are supposed to get done doesn't happen. This is where Mother Nature steps in and starts making her assignments as needed. We've never been left without guidance. It's not what you want, it's what you need [that is important]. Privilege and principle are made for those [of the spirit man] who wish to ascend. [At the Jubilee], all things must be returned – Circle 7, cycle 7. The corporate de facto system is designed to steal Birth Rites.

331. *Rod*: You have to use the morals to conquer the dogma. I'm not here to toot my own horn. I'm not telling everybody about me. This is about the collective. When you come in with a superior jurisdiction, it's like driving a bulldozer through the courthouse. You are coming with a Birth Rites and Blood that is tied to the land with first rights of claim to the land that they cannot interrupt, and they know who we are from the day we were born. People have a one hundred percent right to disagree with everything I have said. There are people who have a hundred percent right to agree with me if they choose to. When I pull up the contracts now, this is the Jubilee. I am number 7 from the 313; born with three sevens in my head because I am the seventh seed of a seventh seed of a seventh seed. With the Blood Rite and the numerical value, they already know that I had the Rite to restore and reclaim the land for the people and for us to get to work restoring our family structures back where all of the clans can end the war like it's supposed to be. We fought to integrate with some people who had nothing to do with us. That is why Nobel Drew Ali needed us to learn civics. If you

don't know civics, you will never know what these people are doing that they ain't got no business doing. You won't know how to get rid of them. The way that I see it, people are looking at nationality is the application to become a national as a diplomatic status under a corporate jurisdiction. They are not looking at a certain nature de jure Birth Rite. So they are trying to use the system and to work within a system that is designed to entrap you at every turn.

332. *Taj*: Nations around the world are now using the principles, not a constitution, but the principles to restore the Republic platforms so [that] they can get back to their organic selves on the land. (Rod: that was the reverse engineering.)
Rod: Before we can assert tribal Rites in the crash site [which is the] ten square miles known as the District of Columbia, we had to first seize the flag of the Amorite jurisdictions and by replacing it with the law of the land by occupying Pelosi's desk with no fringe (that's the law of the land) that is taking you back to the Republic. Now we have to take the ten square miles that the Republic claims and reclaim it as Indigenous by establishing a Totem Pole (Taj: Aboriginal title/claim that supersede all other claims, deeds, or any other instrumentations created under the corporate structure, all of which are dead.). When we posted the Totem Pole to seize D.C., [it is] because that was the only territory that was in dispute. That was the corporate jurisdiction of the United States; everything else outside of that was also assumed jurisdiction that wasn't really operating according to the law of the land. They were operating under Salvage Law, and Amorite jurisdiction. When you have the flag of the land, and then you have the Totem Pole, you put them together, that is the organic

people of the land using their system to overthrow the artificial system that does not belong here.

333. *Taj*: When Noble Drew Ali set up the Moors Temple of Science civic platform (not the Moors Science Temple of America) those things were supposed to be taught to the people so that they could recognize their relationship to what they assumed to be government and discover that in reality that they were not the government and that we had relinquished our responsibility and given up our Birth Rite under ignorance.

Rod: Ignorance likened to making deals with $5 Indians claiming they were us. They brought them over here as P.O.W.s [then] they made agreements with them and replaced us on the Trail of Tears when they assassinated us with 'Paper genocide.' They changed our legal designation in the paperwork, (Andrew Jackson?). When they were doing that it was to confuse all of the outcome. One thing that they cannot get around is the Blood and the Rite. I've got the Blood and the Rite to be the family redeemer for my sisters and all of the sisters that are part and partner to the claim that chose to use me as the family redeemer to redeem the rightful jurisdictional position in natural law and override the Amorite jurisdiction of a de facto corporation. This is a lot of legalese, but we have to know the legalese because that is where they have deceived us the most.

334. *Taj*: This is why it's so important to spend more time teaching and sharing those principles of I/self/law/master. That is the metaphysical principle of Vodun, and not the creed principle of Islam that people assume that is meant. It means I, self, law, and master. That means taking back your lost estate. It has nothing to do with bowing down and praying to nothing. It has to do with re-instating your

connection with nature, the land, and the principles laid down by our forefathers based on our obligation to send those principles back on the land with the people in the culture always being careful that the seventh generation after us is protected with those same principles so that they can be passed down to the next seven in cycles. It is our obligation. So, the women must step up and stop playing this church game that they have been playing for this last hundred years, and get back into their right state of mind, and use that womb properly. Our women are spending so much time being somebody that they are not, and not recognizing that their actions charge [or not] the whole nativity; the nation collective. In order to fix the nation, you have to fix the womb, in order to fix the womb, you have to fix the chambers of heaven which is the mind. We must go back to the metaphysical principles of *Hermetic Law*, and *Laws of Maat*. Birth Rite cannot be sold. If when you are providing a service that has to do with Birth Rite, and you put a lien on it, you are dirty. This is back to people not really overstanding government and corporate entities. We are broken in many ways; spiritually, and culturally. We are broken in the manner of our people participating in political platforms when they don't know politics. We keep voting when we don't know that we are not a part of what we are voting for. We keep fighting to be a part of something that is actually the opposite ward of themselves. The only thing that has to do with us is a faux-fer issue of them being what you call an interregnum faux-fer occupational government who has obligations according to international law which they have breached. Not only that, they are bankrupt and has no business doing any activity whatsoever on any level. However, the people themselves have not stepped up because all of their leadership for the most part has been compromised. Thankfully a few people have stepped up in spite of it all to speak on behalf of the people proper, claiming the estate.

335. *Rod*: The prophet said, when you open your mouth, the assumption of ignorance becomes proven. You can claim to know something, but if you do not know the path to walk, you don't know the questions to raise, you don't know the jurisdictional challenges, then you are just talking. What we are talking about today is, whether I call myself a Moor or not, I'm Growth and Development. I am an Elder, and my job is to compel the people to wake up and see what is going on in front of your face before you get caught in a culture shock of great magnitude when things switch [over] and you were not paying attention. It is the same as when they were trying to tell [the slaves] that they were free in the Juneteenth story. This system is over. You do not have to believe me, but it's going to be proven. And everything I said that I did and gave instructions to be done; seize the Vatican, seize Buckingham Palace, seize the military industrial complex, seize Wall Street, seize the International Monetary Fund, Stock Exchange, the World Bank, all of the corporate holdings, the secret societies that was implicit in the human trafficking network, all of this is already recorded. You all will see, whether you agree with me or not.

336. Taj taught me civics well enough to know what I need to do with the Blood and the Rite to reclaim the land. That was his duty that he received from Noble Drew Ali that was passed to him [via] wind talking on the land, through the land, man to man. He didn't have to sit at the table for Noble Drew Ali [in order to] get his marching instructions. And he did it flawlessly because as he said earlier, I have been watching him say the same thing for fifty years redundantly.

I say he has the patience of a Saint, because they have been asking the same questions for fifty years – no diversity in the questions he is being asked. Therefore he has to keep telling the answers that he gave the day before that, the week before that, the month before that, ten years before that, he has to keep answering the same questions. What does 'black' mean in law, what does 'white' mean in law, what is the de jure position, what is the de facto position. We know all of that now. What we are going to do about it, and do you know what to do about it is where we are at now.

337. Because I studied the civics that Taj taught, I know what Noble Drew Ali said [when he said] "I'm going to leave these people in power long enough for you to learn how to run a government." I can single handedly run the government better than all of these bastards put together. So he must have been talking about now, and he must have been talking about me, because I do not see anyone making the proper claim, in their proper persona, in their proper jurisdiction as the de jure on the land in the face of the de facto government that is an interim government established under false pretenses in conjure magic, Babylonian Blood magic, Babylonian money magic, and Babylonian sex magic, under the Rites of Ninercin – I can take this –ish all the way back to where it started at; they came from Nibiru to Earth (from heaven to Earth), the Nephilims, they came, they fell down, they came down here on Mount Sinai, the mountain of sin, the Holy Mt. Zion of Yahweh, who is Enlil, Lord of the sky who took jurisdiction over Enki, Lord of the Earth. When he did that, he sent his children out to cause mischief and Bloodshed everywhere that they go. There is no right in them because they just don't know how to be right. They are just like their daddy, a no good rotten MF. So, they can be offended by it. They look like us, but they are not us. They

are relatives, but they are not direct relatives. They've got a different agenda. They came to collect the gold, and they wanted us to become their permanent slaves. I don't want to be their slave. So f_ck those mfs, and the ship they rode in on. Vermono, whatever you want to call it – Sham, and they can leave. I got the report today from the Pleiadians that a major event is incoming. And they are running in every corner trying to escape, but there is no escape this time. [Taj: Some of the people continuing the B.S. don't know that the head has already been removed.] Which is also time stamped and dated on my Facebook page when the dragon was beheaded by Inana herself because she said that she was not going to give anybody else the satisfaction, including me. They are no longer under the Archonic rule of Rome. Babylon fell in their faces and they weren't even watching.

338. They are feeding off of the people's ignorance that is keeping the system going; they are vampires. As long as the people are contesting their organic Rites to the Earth, anywhere on the Earth, then the inorganic beings that came here with hostile intentions remains here, but they are in flight mode now. That is the message from the Pleiadians that the reptilians are in flight mode in every direction. They can't go anywhere. They are blocked by Pleiadian light blockers, a form of Metatron's cube. They are caught between the lunar magic and the dark light satellite frequencies; between technology and sorcery. (Tag: if they try to force their way out they will vaporize.) No one is getting out of here without paying for their dirt. The books are open and they have been found wanting.

339. They have not done right by the righteous people of the Earth, so now the righteous people of the Earth have a whole lot of free karma to cash in, and they do not have the means

to pay it, so now they want to run. There is nowhere to run and nowhere to hide. All the Moors know that they have some Dirty Moors, but it is not my job to clean that up. I just had to let you know they were there and that they were trying to undermine the up-lift-ment of all of humanity in search of personal wealth and personal gain.

340. My job is to help Larry Hoover to clean up the nation of Growth and Development, and to help *Big Tookie* to clean up the C-Nation on the west coast. *Angel Bey* and *Tarik Bey* are going to have to lead the effort to clean up the Moors that is not my domain. I have no authority over the Moors. But when I come to read the land, I have to tell them where the infiltrators are at; how Noble Drew Ali went in and found out what the dirty Moors were doing and put it in the public domain, they came in *32 Degrees Scottish Rite Freemasons* under Albert Pike masquerading as George Washington, they established their de facto jurisdiction by shedding the Blood of *Crispus Attucks* to establish the two hundred year contract in 1776, that would have expired in 1976 if anybody would have ended the contract, we knew who the enemy was but we didn't know how to identify them in motion so we watched them for another hundred years. When we made them, we recorded everything they did.

341. The *Secondary Constitution* is written in the Blood of *Crispus Attucks* and it is kept in the Washington Memorial Museum in Washington D.C. When it comes time to clean up the land, it's going to be us – organics from over here. We are going to support our Chiefs. We all have our jobs that was ascribed to us by Big Momma. The rogue elements off the land in all of their corporate capacities. They have outworn their use, they have outlasted the lifetime of their contract which have had multiple extensions; Nobel Drew Ali

gave them some, they got extensions through 1933 bankruptcy, 1963 bankruptcy, it is all on the record.

342. We know about the Bank Act, the Federal Reserve Act, the Internal Revenue Act, they are all just acting. All they are doing is acting because they are not the real ones. We are the real ones. My receipts are all on my Facebook page. Those asking for receipts have not done the background searches for themselves to know where we are at. All of the ships [stalled] outside of the docks that can't come in except one at a time [with] full searches because in the continuity of government, you can't have ships running in willy-nilly unless you get invaded by a foreign force. It is the protocol of transitional government to shut down the docks and export/import has to be to a screeching halt. And we found many ships full of refugees that the U.S. military and National Guard and foreign militaries around the world have collected that were in the human trafficking trade.

343. But we are so busy watching this clown Biden that we do not know what is [really] going on. That is the distraction; the misdirection. The fossil fuels [costs] have to go up because they are operating on their reserves. We have oil stocked pile over here. They haven't been able to trade in oil from the Americans, that is why they are just stock piling them. They can borrow money against it, but they cannot sell it. Their contract says they cannot sell it, and they didn't sell it. All of the minerals they have been shipping around the world, they have been shipping here. We seized *De Beers* for the labor practices in Africa. When the major event, the switch, comes, this is how the wealth will be distributed; anything that you have to dig three feet more [than] beneath the earth to get, has to first satisfy the needs of the local people before it can be exported for anybody's gain

whatsoever. That means, if your country is the country that primarily produces a metal, that metal cannot go anywhere until it satisfies the need of the people within that demarcation; those within its borders. That is the only reason that we are leaving the current system up, because it is good for the distribution of wealth to the Riteful heir within the geographical location of the lines of demarcation set up by the corporation during their military campaign.

344. We just need to get back to organizing our family structures. Who is going to be your family accountant, that is what we need to be worried about; which of you is going to be on your family bank board of directors, because we are going to have to decentralize that if we want to be part and parcel to our own destiny. Decentralizing the banks require us going back to our own family bank. This is the land of Tehuti, the land of the feathers, the bird clans; they f_cked up when they came over here. When you are seeing me, that means [that] –ish got bad. The ones that put us in the condition couldn't remember what they did, so I had to figure it out.

345. Farrakhan said that it is going to be like unscrambling eggs, and asked me if I was up for the challenge. I said, unscrambling eggs is almost impossible, but it ain't impossible, so I tried it. So I unscrambled the eggs; going to the fifth dimensional plane of the fourth, playing 5D chess with the invaders, they lost, we won, checkmate. Farrakhan got files on the enemies. A lot of us don't remember, Malcolm X didn't just die as an opposition to Elijah, he ran a 'red herring.' The murder plot was to get Elijah, but they feared Malcolm more. So Malcolm ran the red herring to draw the heat and told Elijah who all the dirty players were in the public domain. When he ran the dirty players down, we

thought he was just calling names, but he said "the people in the streets know I'm not telling on anybody, the police told me this, this is how I know." Now he is already telling you that the people in the street know he did not tell it. And the reason they know he did not tell it is because they know it and the police know it. The same who murdered Clarence 13X, are the same; and the same ones who slaughtered almost all of Kareem Abdul's family. The same ones who acted like Maltese, and waited till Noble Drew Ali went to sleep and decided to bid him up to Rome (as they call it). They could not get to him pass his Maltese, before they got infiltrated. When Noble Drew Ali got usurped, Elijah Muhammad had to have security, so they came up with something different from the Maltese; they created the *F.O.I.[Fruit of Islam]* security team. A lot of the *S.O.I.* were Nation of Islam before became trainers of the *F.O.I.* If you are trying to build it up, why not use what is already available. The righteous is going to always form our own, [even if it is] from the dirt.

346. When *Farrakhan* opens the books, he's got the names of all the dirty players going all the way back to 1913. When he opens the books, he can call their names out, the living and the dead. He can tell you exactly what they did, who they've done it with, who they made their allegiances with, and who paid them off. Most of them were paid off by Prescott Bush Inc.

Taj: That is why they would never show the people the FBI papers that indicate those who they were controlling with the COINTEL operations which was initiated long before they admitted to it. They admit that they initiated it around 1966; that has been operating around J. Edgar Hoover's time.

347. *Rod*: You have to remember that the same program under a different name is how they deceived and arrested Marcus Garvey. It was the same leadership that put that program together. They are the same ones who paid for the assassination of JFK, Robert Kennedy, Martin Luther King, and John Lenin. The same dirty hands. So when they want him [Farrakhan] to pull out the books, this is what they are talking about, and he is going to it Q: On the June 6th Inquisition, those pale skin who occupied Pelosi's desk, pictured with the Totem Pole looked like $5 Indians. Where is the indigenous people in all of this? We sent the people in that looked like them, the same way that they came in and did us in the beginning is the same way we had to exit. We had to use the same strategy they used to enslave us to get out of slavery; we just had to play it in reverse. There is no secret in who he was trained by because he tells you that he was trained by the shamans that were native to the land, and that he was sent in by the Q-anon. This is before any of the occupation took place because he had to be clearly identified and who he was working for in the public record in the public domain.

348. *Taj*: and people need to know that Q-anon was not set up with Trump, it was set up with Lincoln. Do the best that you can with what you know, and Mother Nature will take care of you. But if you want Rome, then you will go down with them – the right of free Will. Sincerity opens all brains – in the head, heart, and stomach. You will know through your feelings and vibrations. Just be [the best you]. In all you have to do is to start paying attention to the signs and to nature. Nature will tell all that you want to know. All you have to do is to be sincere. Never forget that the church did not come from the Bible, the Bible came from the church. Everything that was built in the 3rd dimensional venue of the Piscean priesthood, it can't survive in the Aquarian light

anyway. The blowing of the trumpet means this on another level: both sound, colors, etc., and vibrations will be used for healing. It is ancient. Where the dark priesthood has been making the people sick, sound and vibration will be used to heal them; to put them back into a vibrational state so that they can ascend. The Will to accept it is your own determination. You have a choice. [At the same time] there will be no choice. The people are going to come together, not because there hasn't been a lack of persons who have risked their personal lives to bring this information to the people [and to light], people will come together out of pain because some people still want this 3rd dimensional experience. [People] will try and imply their responsibility of spiritual development onto others. However, they are not going [to be able] to blame it on others.

Rod: "Weak and insufficient as thou art oh man in good, there is one thing in which you are firm, an obstinate, and its name is misery."

349. Rod: In the [near] future we will be back 5 dimensional frequency vibration meaning higher knowledge, higher wisdom, and higher overstanding and they won't be able to deceive us anymore. It's about the closing of the old Age, the Piscean Age where everything was under water and murky, to the Air Age of Aquarius, which is the moisture of the air. So we are restoring the Shu & Tefnut balance, and we are replacing the Shu/Men resonance back to its proper balance male to female, and taking out the double masculine polarity in the grid that caused us to be in a stupor, called the *Spell of Kingu or the spell of slumber.*[Spell of Kingu=Spell of Leviathan 666 by Malachi York]

350. Once the stupor is broke then we start getting what's called in the modern conscious community, di-flow; Mother

Nature is going to tell you everything that you need to know if you listen to that inner voice. Listen to that inner voice over everything I say, because it's going to tell you what's right, even if I make a mistake. I don't have to always be right. I just have to always tell the truth the best I can. (*Taj; and stay true to the path*).

351. They told me [to] unscramble this egg, it's unscrambled; back in the shell. Humpty Dumpty is back on the wall; unlimited potential that is; so now we are going to let the eagle hatch the egg and see what this unlimited potential produce. This is the coming together of the divine masculine and the divine feminine in a joint effort to put Big Momma back on her Throne. This is where we are at now. We are getting away from all that- you need a dictator to dictate your reality. You have an option to participate in the creation of tomorrow because it isn't here yet. Everybody is going to get what they earn; good, bad, of indifferent. If you reap an unjust reward by being unjust, you are going to get that reward. If you follow the goodness in your heart, and have been the best person you could and pursue the path of righteousness, you are going to get a righteous reward. There is no division. The division is in the ignorance. The knowledge overstands what is taking place, the ignorance is blind to the knowledge. We have been in perpetual war for five hundred years. I came to end the war because after the war you have prosperity. You cannot have war and prosperity at the same time.

> *Come all ye Asiatic of North America, and take your places among the affairs of men... You are the creators and makers of your own* – Noble Drew Ali
>
> *Up ye mighty people! Do as ye Will.* – Marcus Garvey

352. The operative word is 'Will.' It's the 'Law of Use' of the universe that if you are not using your free Will, then your enemy can use it against you. So we are making the connections on the land with the ones who know what to do, in order for the ones who don't know what to do watch us do it so they will know what is necessary for their own enrichment and self-development and development of our people, wherever we are at on Earth. We are native all over the planet; from pole to pole, prime meridian to prime meridian. We've been here, going to be here. Everybody who do not belong here has to go. That is by order of Galactic counsel.

353. The Law Preservation being the first law of nature allows us to come to an agreement with the rogue elements to give them their quota of gold, but they are supposed to give us our quota of technology because they stripped the telomeres [of the chromosomes] back to make us grow old and die. We think death is normal, but it is not. We are supposed to take off this meat suit when we are ready, not when we get broke down and decrepit. We are not supposed to get broke down and decrepit. The life and the science is in med-beds and healing-chambers. This technology has been recently re-discovered by a secret society called the Lazarus Group. As the telomeres on the genes deteriorate, we age. The telomeres use to cover the full chromosome. They [in the past] used science to interrupt our forever time.

354. We are going to hear from Larry Hoover who has to give a report on the land. He has a collective report from all of the Chiefs that address the grievances of the collective. There are no big I's and little U's in this matter. I am no better than anybody, and nobody is better than me. Taj is my Elder, been my Elder, and is going to be my Elder. After

all of the posts that he has held all these years, I have to do my part. I don't have to do his part, he has done his part. I use his part in order to facilitate me in doing my part. [Passing of the baton from 80 year old Elder to the youth.] The same as C. Freeman Hill, who taught me metaphysics from the perspective of the Moors. The same with Hakim Bey who taught me connections of the ones who came verses the ones who are from the land, and how they move within the Moors Science Temple. But that is not my first domain. I'm from the blue house to honor my Father, and I'm from the red house to honor my Mother. I'm not taking sides. But I'm going to clean this –ish up. We don't have to agree on every single point and detail, everybody just have to do their part.

APPENDIX

The Tree of Life

Ancient wisdom can be found in the construct of a tree referred to as a *'mandala.'* Ancient texts reference two different trees; 1) *The Tree of Life*
2) *The Tree of Knowledge*

The Tree Of Life demonstrates the progression of man/woman through spiritual stages of development from birth. Within these ancient writings is a map of pre-recorded knowledge from those who have gone before. Their recorded awareness provides an overstanding of the generalizations of life for helpful navigation.

Starting from the bottom of the tree, (stages 9-7), it is recognized that every human is born with common faculties as instinct, communication, socialization, and imagination. Additional faculties (stages 6-2) may be acquired through increased knowledge and divine awareness. It is beneficial to have an awareness of the faculties of the *Tree Of Life*. It is even more beneficial to learn how to navigate its ascension. Together with proper training and divine inspiration, it is possible for man/woman to reach his/her highest level of consciousness (stage 1).

Study the stages listed below:

Illus.

from
The Return by *Yao Nyamekye Morris*

The Tree of Life

Sphere 1-6 are
attributes of
Higher Self

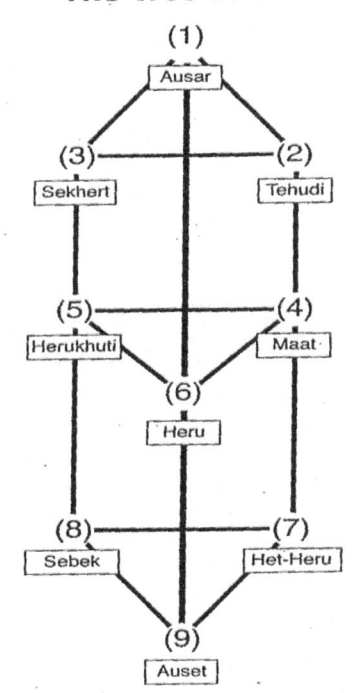

(1) Ausar
(3) Sekhert
(2) Tehudi
(5) Herukhuti
(4) Maat
(6) Heru

Sphere 7,8 & 9
are active at birth

(8) Sebek
(7) Het-Heru
(9) Auset

201

Ausar	Sphere 1 Divinity	Unity. The ability to be one with all things. The "Mummy", a nature so highly evolved, one is immune to all emotional or earthy influences.
Tehudi	Sphere 2 Divine Wisdom	The ability to intuit all knowledge, directly, first hand. "All knowing." The ability to communicate with each faculty of God directly. The level of the sage.
Sekhert	Sphere 3 Divine Power	Control of the life force, the formative base of all things in the world. Governs the cycles of life and death, yin and yang.
Maat	Sphere 4 Divine Truth	The ability to comprehend the natural law. Truth is a measure of how function adheres to form. Do we live according to God's design? The ability to acquire one's needs through an understanding of the laws governing a situation.
Herukhuti	Sphere 5 Justice	The attribute of defense and protection. The use of spiritual power to defend from external attack. The use of spiritual power to heal inside the body, internal attack.
Heru	Sphere 6 The Will	The ability to rise above fears and conditionings, and exercise the will. The use of the will to live truth. The ability to self regulate oneself.
Het Heru	Sphere 7 Harmony, Beauty	The ability to get along with people and things that are different from us. The full manifestation of the seductive aspect of our sexual nature. The ability to attract, physically and spiritually. The employment of the imagination to create.
Sebek	Sphere 8 Language	The faculty that allows us to separate and define the parts of a whole. Our ability to communicate thoughts, but not the act of thinking.
Auset	Sphere 9 Devotion	The faculty of trance. Devotion. The tendency to mimic others. The nurturing instinct.

TREE OF LIFE AFFIRMATIONS:

9) Aset; Devotion (active at birth)

The faculty of trance; nurturing instinct; devotion; the tendency to mimic others.

> *I draw upon intuitive resources for the successful completion of plans and projects. I successfully cultivate talent and abilities with purpose and work. In thought, word, and deed I rest my life upon the Eternal Being. The Kingdom of Spirit is embodied in my flesh.*

❖

8) Sebek; Communication (active at birth)

The faculty that allows us to separate and define the parts of a whole; The ability to communicate thoughts, but not the act of thinking. Communication is one of the three faculties through which our behavior can be reprogrammed at will. Gain knowledge to grow beyond innate instincts. Prepare to make sacrifices for the spiritual awakening of the will and the life force.

> *I formulate and empower mental images of success with desires and emotions that motivate me to achieve. I look forward with confidence to the perfect realization of eternal life.*

❖

7) Het Heru; Harmony and Beauty (active at birth)

The ability to get along with people and things that are different; the full manifestation of a seductive and sexual nature; the ability to attract, physically and spiritually.

> *In all things, great and small, I see the beauty in divine expression. I do not yield to habits and negative behavior that bring pain and suffering.*

❖

6) Heru; The Will

Man's will; the freedom to choose is man's greatest gift from the Creator; the ability to rise above fears and conditionings and exercise the will; the use of the will to live in truth; the ability to self- regulate oneself.

> *Instead of following the emotional compulsions of the human mind, I choose to joyfully activate the Creator's spiritual power within. Living from that will that is supported by unfailing wisdom and overstanding. Mine is a victorious life.*

❖

5) Herukhuti; Justice

The attribute of defense and protection. Our protection from the injustices of others can only come from our beings, the vessels of the Creator's wisdom and spiritual power in the world. This is your power to immediately cut the negative thoughts and emotions that obstruct good attributes from manifesting in your spirit; the use of spiritual power to defend from external attack; the use of spiritual power to heal inside the body from internal attacks.

> *I identify and transform the forces and conditions that attempt to obstruct my progress. I recognize the manifestation of the undeviating justice in all the circumstances of my life.*

❖

4) Maat; Divine Truth

Because we are separated in the inferior part of our being, and united in the superior part, the emotion of unity which is love is the most powerful of all emotions. When we are able to radiate love as a spiritual force, it generates order, peace and harmony within our being and to others in our surroundings. Love is the key to peace and prosperity through cooperation and health; the ability to comprehend natural law. Truth is a measure of how function adheres to form; fidelity to an original standard based upon reality and actuality; the ability to acquire one's needs through an overstanding of the laws governing the situation.

> *I attract the resources that are required to facilitate my growth and development. From the exhaustless riches of limitless substance, I draw all things needful, both spiritual and material.*

❖

3) Sekhert; Divine Power

The Creator provides everyone spiritual power in the absence of help or resources. Control of the life force is the formative base of all things in the world; it governs the cycles of life and death; yin and yang.

Filled with overstanding of its perfect law, I am guided moment by moment along the path of liberation. I perceive the vocation through which my unique energy pattern will find its highest expression.

❖

2) Tehuti; Divine Wisdom

The Creator has made it possible to intuit its word, that we may receive direct guidance in the affairs of our lives; the ability to intuit all knowledge directly, first hand; "All knowing;" the ability to communicate with each faculty of God directly; the level of Sage.

Through me its unfailing wisdom takes form in thought and word. I am fully aware of my innate talents and abilities.

❖

1) Asar; Divinity

The spiritual center of our oneness with the Creator and the creation; absolute emotional impartiality is necessary for the realization of selflessness and transcendental peace; unity; the ability to be one with all things; the "mummy" state; a nature so highly evolved, one is immune to all emotional or earthly influences.

I am a center of expression for the primal will to do good which eternally creates and sustains the universe. All the power that ever was or will be is here now. I am a creative being with unlimited possibilities

Letter to My People

Today, publication rights of many books of old have been assumed by commercial buyers and republished outside of their original dates and publishing information. For example, a current publication date of 2014 may have actually been published in the 19th or early 20th centuries. You must do your due diligence to locate this original publishing information to have a greater overstanding of the importance and validity of the book information presented. Better yet, search out original books in your family attics, at thrift stores, or at yard sales in order to secure and preserve this original and historical data.

Upon an internet search, I have found that the prestigious *Black Indians* by *William Loren Katz* has been categorized as "Juvenile-fiction."Such categorizations occur when information does not conform to the long standing so-called 'main stream' fiction of European institutions that seek to continue to induce the 'slave imbecilic' narrative and control of the organic native peoples of the Americas, particularly 'Black Americans', into a subservient and captive status.

I personally apologize to the generations of youth today who are, as my generation and past generations were, in a state of confusion. It is our collective duty to study, organize, and correct the many errors of the past; late as it may be, better late than never.

REFERENCE BIBLIOGRAPHY

Amen, Ra Un Nefer. *Medu Neter*. Khami Corp., 140 Buckingham Road, Brooklyn NU 11226, 1990.

Cres-Welsing, Frances, MD. *The Isis Papers*. C. W. Publishing, Washington DC. 1991.

Chaisson & McMillan. *Astronomy Today*, 4th ed. Prentice Hall Inc. N. J., 2002.

Clayton, Peter A. *The Rediscovery of Ancient Egypt*. Thames and Hudson Ltd., London. 1982, 1990.

Katz, William Loren. *Black Indians, A Hidden Heritage*. Open Hand Publishing Inc., Seattle WA, 1986.

Katz, William Loren. *The Black West*. Open Hand Publishing Inc., Seattle WA, 1987.

Lewis, Femi. *The Red Summer of 1919 in U.S. Cities*. Humanities, History & Culture. *www.ThoughtCo.com*. Article, updated 2019.

Massey, Gerald. *Ancient Egypt, Light of the World*. Martino Publishing, Mansfield Centre, CT. 2014 republishing of T. Fisher Unwin, Adelphi Terrace, London. 1907.

McCullough, David Willis, edited by, *Chronicles of the Barbarians*. History Book Club, 1271 Avenue of the Americas New York, NY 10020, 1998.

Muhammad, Elijah. *Message to the Blackman In America*. United Brothers Communication Systems, Newport News, Va. 1992.

Myers, Stephanie E. *Invisible Queen, Mixed Ancestry Revealed*. R.J. Myers Publishing and Consulting Company. 2016.

Nathan, Adele. *Building the First Transcontinental Railroad.* Random House Inc., New York. 1950

Plymouth Rock Foundation. *The Pilgrims.* https:plymrock.org. 2019.

Ray, Regina G. *Contemplations In Black.* Amazon, 2021.

Ray, Regina G. *Balance In Black.* Amazon, 2022.

Supreme Design, LLC. *When the World Was Black.* Supreme Design Publishing, Atlanta, GA. 2013.

Trager, James. *The Women's Chronology.* Henry Holt and Company, New York. 1994.

U.S. History. *Second Continental Congress.* www.ushistory.org. May 03, 2022.

Van Sertima, Ivan. *African Presence in Early Europe.* Transaction Books, New Brunswick (USA) and Oxford (UK), 1985.

Van Sertima, Ivan. *They Came Before Columbus,* Random House, New York, 1976.

Williams, Chancellor. *The Destruction of Black Civilization,* Third World Press, Chicago, Illinois, *1987.*

Zucchino, David. *Wilmington's Lie: The Murderous Coup of 1898 and the Rise of White Supremacy*(2021 Pulitzer Prize). Atlantic Monthly Press, January 7, 2020.

ABOUT THE AUTHOR

Regina G. Ray, a native Washingtonian, was raised under the shadow of the Capitol building. It loomed on the horizon at the far end of the street as she walked to and from school each day in her youth. She left Washington D.C. in 1969 at the age of eight with her family, to honor her father's military tours.

Since the graduation of her daughter 35 years later from the prestigious Howard University School of Business, Regina returned home. With much experience from her travels and now 40 year career in healthcare, opportunity made it possible for her to fulfill her dream of settling in one place. In her words, "It is as if I have come full circle."

During the 1990's much time and energy was directed toward a spiritual awakening that placed Regina on a journey seeking the meaning of life. She spent time amongst spiritual groups such as Pine Camp *Ti-chi*, with *Linda Karim*; *Queen Afua's Sacred Women Circle*; the *Hebrew Israelites of Jerusalem of Dimona, Israel*; the *Ancient Egyptian Order of Athens, Georgia*; *Bobby Hemmitt* lectures on YouTube, etc.

Contemplations In Black is a compilation of her best efforts to apply her overstandings and meditations to paper. It contains found responses to questions sought out over 30 years in an effort to alleviate today's youth from re-inventing the wheel, and to ignite imaginations, old and young, to what is possible. This effort has blossomed into this current book being the final installation of a trilogy: *(available @ amazon)*

Contemplations In Black
Balance In Black
The Book of Hayes, The Story of Big Momma, In Black

Previous self-publications include:
A Reasoning to an Exodus
Ras Tafari, A Lineage of Faith
As It Was, So Shall It Be
The Making of a King

Life activities include:
Microbiology, B.S., A.S.C.P., 1984/1985
NAACP Secretary, Henrico County, VA, 1996
Scoutmaster, Troop 732, Robert E. Lee Council, 1998-2005
Unity Day Chairperson for Senator Henry L. Marsh of VA
Sacred Woman of Queen Afua's, Graduate, 2001
Clinical Microbiology Tech 40 years:
Clinical Microbiology Safety Officer 4 years
Clinical Microbiology Supervisor, 13 years
Researcher, Walter Reed Medical Center, 2017-2020
Antique collector, painter, seamstress, vegetable gardening, Skiing, Beach bum, Author, Grandma

Travels:
District of Columbia, Washington, 1961
Fayetteville, North Carolina

Biscoe, Mount Gilead, Eagle Springs
Otis Air Force Base, Cape Cod, Massachusetts, 1969
Boston, Nantucket, Martha's Vineyard
Tyndall Air Force Base, Panama City, Florida, 1974
Sarasota, Orlando
Incirlik Air Force Base, Adana, Turkey, 1976
Izmir, Karamursel, Ankara, Mersin, Tarsus
Athens, Greece, 1977
Ramstein Air Force Base, Germany, 1977
Kaiserslautern, Wiesbaden
Reese Air Force Base, Lubbock, Texas, 1978
New Mexico, Amarillo, Dallas, San Antonio
Lagos & Kaduna, Nigeria, 1988
Richmond, Virginia, 1989
Dimona, Israel, 2003
Tel Aviv, Beer Sheva, Jerusalem, Dead Sea
Cairo, Egypt, 2003
Suitland, Maryland, 2005
Union, New Jersey 2014
Clinton, Maryland 2016